LOVE

· THAT ·

LASTS

For Men

Published in Pasadena, California, by Bethke Writings. Bethke Writings titles may be purchased in bulk for educational, business, fundraising, or sales promotional use. For information, please email info@bethkewritings.com.

Special thanks to Wheelhouse Creative for the book design and to Jeremy Maxfield as editor.

The Library of Congress Cataloging-in-Publication Data is on file with the Library of Congress
ISBN-13: 978-0692858301

How to get the most out of this book

First, thank you. Thanks for reading and being willing to take this journey with your spouse or significant other. We hope these books serve as a catalyst of change, or simply an encouragement to your already strong relationship.

To get the most out of this book, we suggest a few things. First, we want to acknowledge that every marriage is different. There are different needs, nuances, callings, and circumstances. And finding God's good way and rhythm in *your unique marriage* is the fastest way to true joy. And so that means there might be a few suggestions or notes or thoughts in these books that actually don't work very well for you and your wife. And that's ok. You have the permission to adapt and change and use this book in whatever way best serves you both. If there's a suggestion we give that worked great for us, but it didn't for you, forget it. We want these books to serve you, not shame you or make you think you aren't "doing something right" if something doesn't work for you guys.

Also, as you read you'll notice we set these books up to work best on a weekly basis (i.e. one topic per week). But feel free to change that, slow it down, speed it up, etc.

Lastly, the workbook sections mention when the section is meant to be done individually, and also collectively, so keep an eye out for that.

We hope you enjoy taking this journey with us, and we'd love for you to say hi on social media if you're enjoying it or it's an encouragement!

Jeff & Alyssa

PS: Don't forget to watch the corresponding Love That Lasts videos with our twelve sets of mentors while you read along as well. The books are great by themselves, but we envisioned them working best alongside the video series. If you don't know what that is, Alyssa and I had the chance to interview twelve sets of married mentors who are experts on a particular topic (some you might know like Korie and Willie Robertson from *Duck Dynasty* or Drs. Les and Leslie Parrott). If you don't have the videos and you'd like to get them, visit lovethatlasts. co/video. You will also receive a code to take the Deep Love assessment, which is a custom ten-page report on your relationship. Also use code "videoseries" at lovethatlasts.co/video to take 25% off as a thank you.

SUBSCRIBE
TO OUR
LOVE THAT LASTS
PODCAST

---

lovethatlasts.co/podcast

Theology
of
Marriage

01

There's a cartoon I see on Facebook from time to time of a guy standing on a pile of wooden ladders (similar looking to a pile of firewood), trying to peer over a wall. The point of the image is to highlight the complete ridiculousness of standing on ladders to look over the wall, instead of using the ladder for what it's actually created to do.

A lot of times that's what we do with a healthy marriage and relationship. Without properly understanding what marriage or a relationship is *for*, we can't truly live within the depths of joy it is supposed to provide.

This was a huge topic of conversation for us when Alyssa and I were dating. We'd have long talks, usually over coffee or chipotle, about what we believed relationships and dating to be. Often things came up that we disagreed on, or had different views on, or just maybe didn't even know what we believed.

But one of the things we very quickly made clear was that relationships were for a purpose. We are both followers of Jesus (some of you reading this maybe aren't, and that's ok!), and so for us that meant we believed that marriage was actually bigger than ourselves. The coming together of male plus female in a covenant until death is a picture of sorts. An arrow pointing to something greater.

To truly understand the why of marriage, we have to go back to the very beginning in the Bible (Genesis 1:27-28). When God breathed life into skin and bones and flesh.

So God created man in his own image,

in the image of God he created them;

male and female he created them.

And God blessed them. And God said to them, "Be fruitful and multiply and fill the earth and subdue it, and have dominion over the fish of the sea and over the birds of the heavens and over every living thing that moves on the earth."

I find it interesting, at least in twenty-first century Western evangelicalism, that we individualize *image of God*. While we are all personally made in God's image, notice that when it shows up, it's actually in the context of two parts—male and female. The image of God is not just in the two individuals but it's in their togetherness in a covenant when they become *one image*.

What if we really believed that about marriage? What if we had that high of a view of marriage? For us that makes all the difference. Alyssa and I realize that our many differences aren't actually things to divide over, but rather opportunities to blend together into a fuller image of God.

What it all comes down to in marriage is usually not in the what or the how, but in the *why*. What you believe about marriage is what will show up in the day to day, and define the hopefully 50+ years of you as a couple.

For example, just the other day Alyssa and I got into what we call a "tiff." (What does that even mean? Ha!) I can't even remember what it was about. Like usual, it was probably about something small like which way the toilet paper faces, or whose turn it is to pick up the dog poop in the backyard (who am I kidding, in our family, it's *always* my turn for that one). And in the disagreement or moment of frustration, we have a simple decision to make. We can either believe we are totally right and the other person is stupid and wrong and we can't believe they think that or do it that way. Or we can believe that the differences between us aren't about one side winning or losing, but usually about both drawing each other into the middle. And that was the reminder we gave each other in the middle of the disagreement. We aren't fighting *against* each other; we are fighting *for* each other. This is how we grow more into the people God created us to be.

The day-to-day frustrations in marriage, and the exposing of each other's weaknesses and differences, is actually God's way of making a full picture of Himself in us as a couple. It's like two pieces of sandpaper. At first they are both gritty and rough and can do some serious damage. But if you continually rub them together, they will continue to not only smooth the other piece out, but they become smooth as well. The tension and friction, if dealt with properly, actually creates a new and better image.

But marriage isn't just about being a new image as a couple. It's also about gardening. Just after God blessed them and breathed life into them, He gave them the very first command.

Think about how important this one must be. It's literally the first time God gives direction to the image bearers in the garden. What is He going to say?

"The Lord God took the man and put him in the garden of Eden to work it and keep it. And the Lord God commanded the man, saying, 'You may surely eat of every tree of the garden, but of the tree of the knowledge of good and evil you shall not eat, for in the day that you eat of it you shall surely die'" (Genesis 2:15-17).

The first thing God did was make the image bearers gardeners. He told them to work and take care of the garden.

His first command wasn't *be holy, or listen to worship music, or don't have tattoos.*

It was *to garden.*

Or to put it another way, God told them to go out into the world and take raw materials and make something beautiful. Isn't that what a gardener does? They take raw materials (dirt, seed, water, etc) and they put them together and make something beautiful. Make something that gives others nourishment and life. And that's metaphorically what every marriage is called to do to this day.

Go out into the world and take raw materials and make something beautiful. And when we do that, we are reflecting and living into our identity as image bearers. We are made by the Creator, so it only makes sense to create.

And so a marriage at its core is a team of sorts. Two individuals coming together that are actually more powerful and creative than if they were just individuals. And as a team, they go out into the world and create beauty, do justice, love mercy.

Practically this can mean stopping to talk to your neighbors outside. Pitching in to buy a crib for a friend who can't afford it. Helping out at the local community center. Cooking good meals that bring people together at a table for joy and laughter and life. Meeting with a younger couple and asking them how you can help them or serve them or come alongside them.

Honestly, there is no right answer. You simply ask the question, *How are me and my spouse uniquely gifted and placed to live our lives generously and lovingly for other people?* And when you live out that question, marriage simply becomes more than just about us or puppy-love feelings. It becomes a covenant in which two gardeners go out into the world looking for what they can make more beautiful and more just and more loving.

Let love and faithfulness never leave you;
bind them around your neck, write them
on the tablet of your heart.
Proverbs 3:3 (NIV)

GUIDEBOOK

*Theology
of
Marriage*

"HAVEN'T YOU READ," [JESUS] REPLIED, "THAT HE WHO CREATED THEM IN THE BEGINNING MADE THEM MALE AND FEMALE," AND HE ALSO SAID, "FOR THIS REASON A MAN WILL LEAVE HIS FATHER AND MOTHER AND BE JOINED TO HIS WIFE, AND THE TWO WILL BECOME ONE FLESH? SO THEY ARE NO LONGER TWO, BUT ONE FLESH. THEREFORE, WHAT GOD HAS JOINED TOGETHER, LET NO ONE SEPARATE."

Matthew 19:4-6 (CSB)

Those words are among the most familiar yet sacred realities echoed from one generation to the next. Chances are, you heard it right between "I do" and "you may now kiss the bride!" Most wedding ceremonies conclude with Jesus' words: "What God has joined together, let no one separate."

To highlight the unique nature of marriage, Jesus pointed all the way back to the first pages of Scripture and the first moments of human history. The Bible begins and ends with marriage: Adam and Eve in Genesis, Jesus and His church in Revelation.

In fact, if you could summarize the Bible succinctly, it would be about God creating, pursuing, and restoring a bride—a people for Himself, called into oneness with Him and with each other.

You read in the previous pages that you are created in the image of God and that marriage is a picture of God's love. It's the closest thing you can experience in this world to the joy and satisfaction of God's unconditional goodness.

So, before digging into the specific topics addressed in this workbook, some groundwork needs to be done in order to experience the joy of a flourishing marriage. Each week, we're going to start this section of the workbook with the words of Jesus. If we want to know joy, and flourishing, and beauty, it comes from him. He reveals the truth to us—the truth about who God is and about who we are—who we were created to be.

Write your favorite quote, song lyric, or Bible verse related to love or marriage. If you're extra artistic, get creative with your handwriting or draw something to represent love.

Is she *the* one? Yes and no.

First of all, there is no fairytale relationship. You're no Prince Charming. There's no slaying the dragon and riding into the sunset with your princess as the credits roll. Nobody is perfect and sometimes life is kind of boring, right? You'll have plenty of days filled with doing chores, paying bills, and wondering what that funny smell is—and finding joy is what life is really about. Life doesn't fade into happily ever after once you say, "I do." The closest life gets to a rom-com is when you have the ability to laugh at and learn from your mistakes, finding the joy in the ordinary parts of your life.

This shouldn't be depressing. It's actually more romantic to recognize that out of everyone in the world, you chose your wife and she chose you! You weren't fated for the one (and you don't have to wonder if you found the one, which is one of the most dangerous ideas in our culture). You said, *You're the one I give my love to from this day on.* Choosing— and keeping that promise to continue choosing—to love someone for the rest of your life is crazy romantic. It's a commitment, not just for those beautiful moments of richer and better and in health, but in the mundane and even painful moments too. *Until death do you part.*

So if you are asking yourself the question that our culture is obsessed with, *Is she the one?* think about the simple counsel summed up in a tweet from John Piper.

How to know if you are married to the right person. Short answer: Look at the name on the marriage certificate.

Love is commitment. You choose it every day. And nothing is as satisfying (and as sexy) as a no-matter-what kind of love.

Think back to when you got married.

- **What is your favorite memory of the proposal?**

_____

_____

_____

- **How did you know she was the one?**

_____

_____

_____

- **What is your favorite memory of the wedding?**

_____

_____

_____

- **What is your favorite memory of your first days together as husband and wife?**

_____

_____

_____

- What are some of the normal, everyday lessons you had to learn about life together?

  _____

  _____

  _____

  _____

- Think back over your vows. You may have written your own or used something more traditional, but think about these ideas: _for better, for worse, for richer, for poorer, in sickness and health ..._

  _____

  _____

  _____

- What is something that you love about your wife even more now than you did before getting married?

  _____

  _____

  _____

- What is the hardest thing you've faced together?

  _____

  _____

  _____

- How did you grow from it?

_____

_____

_____

- What is the best thing you've experienced together?

_____

_____

_____

- If you wrote your own vows, think back to what you chose to say. Why did you want to be sure to say those things?

_____

_____

_____

_____

- What is something that you love about your wife even more now than you did before getting married?

_____

_____

_____

_____

First Corinthians 13 is often called the love chapter, so there's a good chance that someone read it aloud at your wedding. A friend of ours, Derwin Gray, who is in the *Theology of Marriage* video with his wife, Vicki, has a great way to encourage people to really meditate (or *marinate,* as he would say) on true, biblical, Christ-like, no-matter-what love. As a pastor, Derwin personalizes this chapter, asking people to use their names every time it says *love.* Try it out!

- **Write your name in the blanks below.**

_____ is patient, _____ is kind.
　　　　　{ love }　　　　　　　　　　　　*{ love }*

_____ does not envy, is not boastful, is not arrogant,
　　　　　{ love }

is not rude, is not self-seeking, is not irritable, and does not keep a record

of wrongs. _____ finds no joy in unrighteousness but
　　　　　　　　{ love }

rejoices in the truth. _____ bears all things, believes
　　　　　　　　　　　{ love }

all things, hopes all things, endures all things.

1 Corinthians 13:4-7 (CSB)

Your marriage ultimately isn't about you. When people see
you, they will get a glimpse of the greatest love—Jesus.
We know what love is because we know who Love is.

That sounds great, but if you're anything like me, then you know a lot of those things aren't always true about yourself. You're not always patient or kind. Sometimes you are selfish and irritable and jealous. But think about how amazing this is: Remember how we said at the beginning that as men and women created in the image of God, our love is a reflection of His love for us? Read back through those same verses but put the name *God* in each blank.

Are you starting to understand God's love for you? Are you starting to see how when your eyes are opened to this all-encompassing and perfect love, your view of marriage and of your spouse is radically transformed. It's like the light has just been turned on and you are seeing the infinite possibilities for loving and for being loved. When you open yourself up, allowing the love of God to fill your heart, it will spill over in the way you love others—especially your spouse. Your marriage will become a picture of God's love for all to see.

Remind yourself of those verses all week. Maybe you want to start each morning by reading these verses as a prayer. Make reminders around your home, in your car, or on your phone. These are great verses to memorize. (Any of the proverbs or words of Jesus you will read each week are great to memorize too.)

**"WHEN OVER THE YEARS
SOMEONE HAS SEEN YOU
AT YOUR WORST, AND KNOWS
YOU WITH ALL YOUR
STRENGTHS AND FLAWS, YET
COMMITS HIM- OR HERSELF
TO YOU WHOLLY, IT IS A
CONSUMMATE EXPERIENCE.
TO BE LOVED BUT NOT
KNOWN IS COMFORTING BUT
SUPERFICIAL. TO BE KNOWN
AND NOT LOVED IS OUR
GREATEST FEAR. BUT TO BE
FULLY KNOWN AND TRULY
LOVED IS, WELL, A LOT LIKE
BEING LOVED BY GOD. IT IS
WHAT WE NEED MORE THAN
ANYTHING. IT LIBERATES US
FROM PRETENSE, HUMBLES
US OUT OF OUR SELF-
RIGHTEOUSNESS, AND FORTIFIES
US FOR ANY DIFFICULTY LIFE
CAN THROW AT US."**

- Tim Keller,
from *Meaning of Marriage*

JOIN
TOGETHER

Make this time together each week special—it's a date night! Turn off your phones and give all of your attention to each other.

- Ask each other about the things you read and wrote about in the "on your own" section on the previous pages. Remember that this is a conversation with your wife. Enjoy it! This exercise each week isn't about interviewing your spouse or checking answers; it's about getting to know each other and developing a habit of meaningful time together.
- Go to *Love That Lasts* in your library at *bethkeworkshops.com* and watch this week's video: Theology of Marriage with Derwin and Vicki Gray. Then, ask each other what was most interesting, most challenging, and your big takeaway from the video. Use the video sidebar to take notes and to help your conversation.
- Plan another night this week to invite a couple over for dinner, ideally an older couple or friends who have been married longer than you have. Share with them that you may be asking them questions as you go through this series. Reading the book, watching the videos, completing the workbook, and talking to friends or mentors will help you see your relationship through different eyes.

> *Proverbs 15:22 says, "Without counsel plans fail, but with many advisers they succeed." Obviously, you want the best marriage possible, so invite others into this experience—and into your life beyond the time it takes you to go through this workbook.*

Theology of Marriage with

Derwin & Vicki Gray

This section is a place to take notes if you also purchased the 12 corresponding video sessions from our 12 mentors. What did they say that resonated with you? What was your favorite part? What was most challenging?

If you don't have this video
you can purchase it at

lovethatlasts.co/videoseries

Trust

I don't get nervous or anxious often, if at all. My demeanor is much more of a "it'll play out however it plays out" type of mindset. But I was seriously nervous during one date in particular with Alyssa.

It was back in 2009 when Alyssa and I had dating for a few months. For some background on our relationship, I was Alyssa's first real boyfriend (the first guy she ever held hands with). I, on the other hand, had made some seriously poor decisions in high school and college in regards to relationships. So after I started following Jesus in college, I had to begin the tough work of healing from the past, reconciliation, and the journey of new creation. But that meant if I was going to seriously pursue Alyssa, I had to properly honor and respect her by telling her about my past and my journey the past few years. All of it.

For me it was about her knowing what she was getting into and also setting a foundation of trust and transparency. But I specifically wanted to tell her early on in the relationship, because sometimes the other person can find out stuff that makes them uneasy about the relationship, but they feel they are already too invested to break up. So I knew after a few months of getting to know each other, it was time for a serious talk so she could make the decision of whether or not she felt comfortable moving forward in a relationship with me.

But, man, I was nervous. Like sweaty-palms, struggling-to-breathe nervous. But I knew I was doing the right thing.

So as we sat in the parking lot of a grocery store, I let it all out. I was honest and vulnerable and, in many ways, scared. But I'll never forget the next moment. Alyssa looked me right in the eyes and said, "That doesn't change how I feel about you. I still want to be with you."

I remember feeling so loved in that moment. When vulnerability and love meet, trust is formed.

Looking back, that was a defining moment for us. Alyssa and I trust each other beyond belief, and it can be traced back to that moment. Someone being honest and vulnerable, and the other person saying thank you and giving love.

We realized that a non-negotiable in our relationship is transparency and honesty. It's each person's job to be honest, and it's on the other person for how they react. But too many times we don't tell our spouse something because we wonder, *How will they react?* But that part is between them and Jesus. All we can do is be honest, but the amount of joy and life brought to a relationship when there is a bedrock of trust is incredible.

Never once in our relationship have I second-guessed her, not trusted her, or felt like I was being lied to. We committed at that time to never do that. And sometimes that means I share with her thoughts I'm struggling with, or how I'm really feeling when I'd rather not or even when it might hurt her. But it's those moments each day that create the foundation of trust and intimacy.

You can't have intimacy if you don't have trust. And trust is something that's lost quickly but built slowly. So wherever you're at in your relationship, whether promises have been broken or you are starting out great, commit to the long road of trust. A healthy relationship can't survive without it.

Write your favorite quote, song lyric, or Bible verse related to trust. If you're extra artistic, get creative with your handwriting or draw something to represent trust.

GUIDEBOOK

Trust

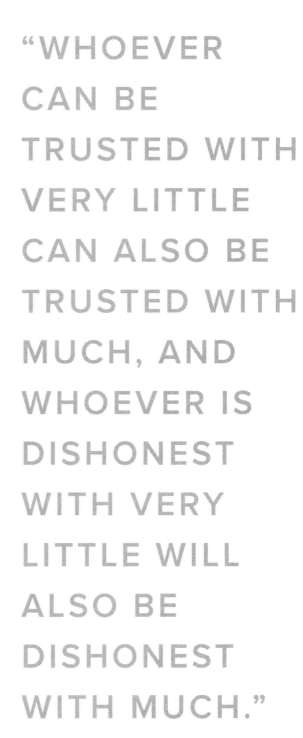

"WHOEVER CAN BE TRUSTED WITH VERY LITTLE CAN ALSO BE TRUSTED WITH MUCH, AND WHOEVER IS DISHONEST WITH VERY LITTLE WILL ALSO BE DISHONEST WITH MUCH."

Luke 16:10 (NIV)

Trust is the key ingredient for any healthy relationship. You have to know that you can trust someone if you're ever going to move beyond a surface-level acquaintance. You may be the kind of person who opens up quickly; however, most people are slow to open up. Whether you dive in headfirst or you gradually test the waters, inching in a little bit deeper over a longer period of time, our hearts have been shaped by God for meaningful relationships.

Jesus told a parable about different servants who had been trusted with different investments from their master. He actually told a few variations of this story that you can read in Luke 16, 19, and Matthew 25. The point to the parables of talents and managers is about making wise decisions based on what you've been given. Ultimately, Jesus is referring to the gospel and our relationship with God. Are we taking what we know about God and valuing his blessings enough to do whatever we can to grow in relationship with Him? To make this point Jesus uses what we all know to be true—some people can be trusted with more than others and if you can't trust someone with simple things, you're crazy if you trust them with something of real value.

The principle of trustworthiness applies to every relationship, not just to your relationship with God and with your wife. Actually, they're going to all bleed into one another like a watercolor. There are no solid lines. There's no compartmentalizing trust into different areas. That's exactly what Jesus is saying about being faithful and trustworthy with a little and a lot. If you can't be trusted with friends or coworkers, how can you be trusted in a marriage? Below is an easy, but hopefully helpful, trustworthiness quiz. There is no failing this test, but it is helpful to truly self assess how much trust you are building with your spouse.

USING A SCALE OF 1-10
(1 = NEVER, 10 = ALWAYS)

Answer the following questions.

How often do you remember to do what you say you'll do?

1 · 2 · 3 · 4 · 5 · 6 · 7 · 8 · 9 · 10

How often do you work hard?

1 · 2 · 3 · 4 · 5 · 6 · 7 · 8 · 9 · 10

How often do you make comments or talk about other people?

1 · 2 · 3 · 4 · 5 · 6 · 7 · 8 · 9 · 10

How often do you laugh at or make jokes about other people?

1 · 2 · 3 · 4 · 5 · 6 · 7 · 8 · 9 · 10

How often do people tell you secrets or personal things?

1 · 2 · 3 · 4 · 5 · 6 · 7 · 8 · 9 · 10

How often do people ask for your advice?

1 · 2 · 3 · 4 · 5 · 6 · 7 · 8 · 9 · 10

If you struggle with the small things like remembering things, making comments and jokes about people, working hard, you may want to dismiss them as not being a big deal, but they actually play into how other people see you and possibly even how they see the value of Jesus. The love of Jesus should transform our relationships.

What do you need to work on in order to be trustworthy in the small things?

_____

_____

_____

_____

_____

Now think about the big things like being dishonest, hurtful, selfish, or unfaithful, and whether or not you are more or less trustworthy than you were in the past. Ask yourself what your attitudes and actions reveal about how much you value the gift of real relationships.

Think about a time that you were really hurt in a relationship. Think about a time when you've hurt somebody else. How have those experiences had a ripple effect in other relationships? Have you grown from those painful betrayals or have the caused you to be guarded?

_____

_____

_____

_____

_____

When you keep other people at a distance, it's the result of sin—either sin around you, within you, or both. Sin makes you hide. That's what you saw in the Garden of Eden (see Genesis 3). Adam and Eve sin, betray God's trust, try to hide, then make excuses and pass the blame to avoid the truth. By the way, how crazy is it to hide behind a tree from the Creator of heaven and earth? He knows *everything!*

That's actually exactly why God's infinite love for us is greater than any-thing we can fully wrap our finite minds around. He knows us *completely.* And yet even while knowing everything he loves us *completely.*

To really experience love means we have to know and be known. It requires honesty. We can't love someone we don't know. We can't be loved if we're putting up a fake image of who we really are. And it's out of being loved by God that we're able to love others.

As man and woman, husband and wife, created in the image of God, the person on this planet that you should trust the most is your wife. She should be able to trust you more than anyone else. Marriage should be a safe place where you can be transparent and vulnerable— naked and unashamed, literally and figuratively.

It's good to have other close friends, people who know you, people you trust, but no other friendship should be more honest and transparent than your marriage. Nobody should know you or your wife better than you know each other. Don't believe the lie that there are some things you just can't tell her.

Trust is key to any *healthy* relationship. If you want your marriage to flourish, you have to be trustworthy and to trust in the little and the big things. You've committed your life to her. She's committed her life to you. That's as big as it gets!

BEFORE YOUR DATE NIGHT DISCUSSION, DO TWO THINGS:

1. Get one of her favorite candies. You will surprise each other with a blind taste test; so keep it covered in a box or bag until you meet!

2. Think about some specific examples of ways that she has shown her trustworthiness—little and big things. Write them here.

_____

_____

_____

_____

_____

_____

_____

_____

_____

_____

_____

Intimacy is based on trust. True intimacy involves an exchange. Someone gives vulnerability, and the other person gives assurance and honor of that vulnerability back. Then reciprocation of that vulnerability happens, creating a beautiful cycle. And that bond is exclusive and hidden, only for the two to behold and be a part of.

JOIN
TOGETHER

Remember to turn off your phones and to give all of your attention to each other. Paying attention instead of being distracted by a phone, TV, etc. is a simple way to be trustworthy in a little thing. You are showing that you value one another.

- Sit together on the couch or at the table. Take turn closing your eyes while your wife gives you a taste of the candy she chose for you. No peeking and no wedding-cake-smashed-in-the-face shenanigans. This is about trust! Try to guess what kind of candy you tasted.
- Ask each other the following questions:

  → Were you nervous about blindly trusting me? Why? What made you believe or doubt that you could trust me in something fun like this?

  → In general, is trusting easy for you? Why?

  → Why do you trust me?

  → What are some of the little things that I do or that I can do that show you that I love you completely?

  → Is any topic of conversation or openness about something in your life strictly off limits when talking to a trusted friend or mentor? (It's important for you both to know what the expectation is here so that you never have a misunderstanding of breaking trust with one another.)

  → Do we need to stop criticizing, gossiping about, or making fun of other people? Do we ever try to justify gossip as concern, prayer requests, or normal conversation?

  → How does having a loving and trusting marriage encourage you to grow in your relationship with God? How can setting an example of trustworthiness in speech and action show others the love of Christ?

- Ask each other about any of the other things you read and wrote about in the "on your own" section on the previous pages. Remember, this is a conversation with your wife. Enjoy it!

- Go to *Love That Lasts* in your library at *bethkeworkshops.com* and watch this week's video: Trust with Melanie and Seth Studley. They have a pretty incredible story of almost divorcing, even though one of them was a marriage and family licensed counselor. They also host a marriage podcast called Stronger Marriages. After watching, ask each other what was most interesting, most challenging, and a big takeaway from the video. Use the video sidebar to take notes and to help your conversation.

- Pray together, thanking God for blessing you with a relationship with him and with one another. Ask for God's help in being thoughtful and trustworthy in everything you do out of gratitude for the gift of love.

A gossip betrays a confidence, but a
trustworthy person keeps a secret.
Proverbs 11:13 (NIV)

Trust with

Melanie & Seth Studley

This section is a place to take notes if you also purchased the 12 corresponding video sessions from our 12 mentors. What did they say that resonated with you? What was your favorite part? What was most challenging?

_____

_____

_____

_____

_____

_____

_____

_____

_____

_____

_____

_____

_____

_____

If you don't have this video
you can purchase it at

lovethatlasts.co/videoseries

Communication

03

Alyssa and I were both sitting on the couch one evening when she nicely asked me to get something from the bedroom for her. Me, being selfish and tired and grumpy that night, decided to ask, "Why don't you go get it yourself"? Which then quickly escalated into each other being upset and rude to each other. I later apologized and felt so dumb, because it was the tiniest thing. And my reaction was not the tiniest thing.

At that moment I remembered a phrase from some of our married friends. A few weeks prior we were at dinner talking about marriage advice when one of them said, "Bring up little things in a little way, and big things in a big way." It's simple, but sadly overlooked. Looking back on our relationship, so many petty arguments or breakdowns of communication have happened because our frustration about something wasn't proportional to the actual issue at hand.

So after our fight that night, Alyssa and I made a commitment to that principle, and it has made all the difference. What it does is give us an excuse to bring up the little things in a little way *before* they turn out to be big things. Because a lot of times what will happen is something small will happen that hurt our feelings or upset us, and we think, "Oh, that's no big deal. I need to get over it." But if gone unsaid, that starts to add up and then later creates a very much disproportional response that makes things worse. Instead, we have committed to saying in the little things, "Hey, that little comment hurt me." Or, "Not a huge deal, but I just wanted to let you know, that I feel overlooked today." Or, "When I asked you to do something, it means a lot when you do, especially after a long day taking care of the kids." However you may say it, make it proportional.

Because we haven't been married that long, Alyssa and I are always looking for other couples to get advice from. One of the things I've noticed is that all the couples I look up to have one thing in common—they all communicate really well. And over the last 7 years with Alyssa, I've learned that communication isn't just a factor in how well your relationship is doing; it is *the* factor. Bad communication creates a bad relationship. Good communication creates a good relationship. This is true at least within our own marriage.

One thing vital to good communication is the ability to come to decisions that are satisfactory for both people. Or, to put it another way, one thing a relationship can't live without is mutual compromise. Alyssa and I have to work hard at this. As a teenager and into my college years, I wanted to be a lawyer. I had a natural inclination for debate, logic, reason, and thinking outside the box. But just like any personality trait, a blessing can also be a curse. Without love, grace, and compassion, I could sometimes be mean without even knowing it. I could be all about the facts, not realizing my words also could hurt other people.

Through time I've come to realize it's not just about what you say but also how you say it. And also, in a marriage, I've realized the mentality of needing to win is poison. Complete poison and it can destroy any relationship. Alyssa and I have both committed to throwing the "I need to win" attitude in the trash because a relationship isn't about winning; it's above love and growing.

So for us, we've committed to compromising. And not compromising to appease the other person, but compromising to love the other person. For example, I hate making the bed. I think it's the worst thing ever and so unnecessary because it's just going to get messed up again later that day when you go to sleep. But guess what? Alyssa *loves* the bed being made every day. To her, it's a great way to start the day and make things feel fresh and orderly first thing in the morning.

This was a huge ongoing conflict for us in the first year of marriage. But finally, I realized I was being dumb, so I decided to forget how I feel and my preferences. I want to serve my wife, and this is one small way of doing that. And the beautiful thing is that act of service then warmed Alyssa's heart and spurred her on to serve me back in a myriad of other ways. Service is contagious and creates a beautiful cycle. And usually it starts with compromising.

Agree as a couple to compromise on some stuff and be sensitive to what that might be for each other, because "bending is better than breaking" as a famous quote so rightly puts it about compromise.

No one knows what it means to be intimate anymore and not just in our sexuality but platonically speaking as well. It's why whenever I'm out with friends and there's an awkward silence, we pull out the phone. We look down. We don't know what it means to be known anymore. In fact, I think we are terrified of being known, not realizing that's exactly where joy is hiding.

GUIDEBOOK

Communication

LET YOUR "YES" MEAN "YES," AND YOUR "NO" MEAN "NO."

Matthew 5:37 (CSB)

Sometimes the most profound truths are the most obvious. Jesus' simple command 2000 years ago is just as countercultural and challenging today:

Say what you mean. Do what you say.

Jesus is saying that if you have to add all kinds of promises or conditions to convince someone to believe you, then your words don't mean very much. The issue isn't whether or not it's OK to "swear" or to take oaths. The point Jesus is making is that character matters. Your words, your attitude, and your actions should all be sending the same message. People should know that you always keep your word.

The saying "actions speak louder than words" doesn't mean that words don't matter. It means that they only matter if you also do what you say. There's another Christian cliché that sounds similar: "Preach the gospel at all times and, when necessary, use words." The point, I think, is that everything we do communicates what we believe. It's not enough to say you love Jesus, if you don't act like it. It's not enough to say you love your wife, if you don't act like it.

But in your effort to remember that actions speak loudly, don't forget that the Good News of Jesus absolutely requires using our words. It's good news, right? Not just a good attitude. Following Jesus and sharing the gospel is about a lot more than just being nice.

In the same way, loving your wife is about a lot more than being nice. You have to show her, tell her, talk to her, listen to her, spend time with her, pay attention to her … you get the idea.

Write your favorite quote, song lyric, or Bible verse related to the power of words or connecting with people in a meaningful way. Draw a picture. Or write a poem or song this week, expressing yourself creatively.

There are a lot of ways to communicate. All of them are important. All of them should echo the same message, like different instruments playing in harmony to create one song. And your song will be stuck in her head on repeat—hopefully, it's a love song that she sings without even realizing it while she goes throughout her busy day. Your song should make her dance. Your song should make her smile. Your song should give her comfort.

- **Do you and your wife have "a song"? What is it? What other song or song title would be a good summary of your relationship?**

_____

_____

_____

_____

_____

- **What makes that song, uniquely special? Is it the lyrics? Is it a memory associated with the song? Is it the mood of the music?**

_____

_____

_____

_____

_____

- If you were to create a playlist for your life together, what songs would you add to the mix? What songs would she add?

  _____   _____

  _____   _____

  _____   _____

  _____   _____

  _____   _____

- Music is just one way people creatively connect with one another. What are other ways people can creatively connect with each other?

  _____

  _____

  _____

- How do you best express yourself?

  _____

  _____

  _____

- What kinds of things do you do to let your wife know that you love her?

  _____

  _____

  _____

- **How does your wife express herself?**

_____

_____

_____

Now here's the key: Do you express yourselves in the same way? If not, you may think you're communicating with your wife and letting her know that you love you her, and she may think she's communicating with you, but it's like you're speaking different languages.

For example, if Alyssa likes spending time together and I'm like a big kid who likes new gadgets, I may think that buying her little gifts is a great way to express my love for her, when what she wants is to go for a walk through the neighborhood. I may want to build her a new piece of furniture when she wants us to play together with the kids. Does that make sense? They're all good things, but we're not communicating well.

You know those embarrassingly awkward moments when someone can't speak a foreign language so they just speak louder? They may even speak slower or with an accent, like somehow being loud and slow and using a bad accent is going to help someone suddenly understand a different language. It's ridiculous and offensive.

That's what it's like sometimes in marriage. A spouse can get frustrated and feel neglected or misunderstood. No matter how hard they try, things only get more awkward or tense as both people stubbornly continue to repeat their own ways of doing things. Don't be that guy. Learn what is meaningful to her and start speaking her language.

You've already seen that trust is vital for healthy relationships. Communication is a major part of developing trust and intimacy. Your wife has to know that when you say something, you mean it. She also has to believe that when she says something, you get it. She needs you to not only hear her, but to also understand her. You're listening. Real communication is happening, not just talk. No agenda. No saying one thing and meaning another. No guessing games.

Do you ever feel misunderstood?	**YES	NO**
Do you ever have trouble understanding your wife?	**YES	NO**
Do you always say what you mean?	**YES	NO**
Do you always do what you say?	**YES	NO**
Do you actually listen?	**YES	NO**

While we're on the subject of sending and receiving mixed signals, let's think about some other ways we communicate. Think back to the relationship between your actions and our words. All of these things are important in communicating well.

- What you say.
- When and where you say it.
- Why you say it.
- How you say it.
- What you do about it.

Do this quick exercise to think about how the truth can be clearly communicated or get lost in translation.

Your wife comes home after a bad day. She really wants to talk about it. You've had a tough day too, but really don't want to talk about it. Give an example in each of these categories of the right and wrong way to communicate.

COMMUNICATION	GOOD	BAD
WORDS		
TIMING		
INTENT		
TONE		
BODY LANGUAGE		
ACTIONS		

The goal of communication should be connection. Communication should build trust and intimacy. It's about the other person as much as or more than it is about you. Be intentional this week to pay attention to how you interact with your wife. Make sure you're not sending mixed messages with the different ways you communicate. This is essential to not only the rest of this workbook, but more important, to the rest of your relationship. Be sure that she knows you love her.

Remember to give all of your attention to each other, but you may want your phone to get started this time. That's up to you. You may normally have music playing in the background or you may not. This week it could be fun to have some music. Whatever you do, take clear action to demonstrate your love for one another by prioritizing this time together. If playing music, let it enhance the experience, not distract from it.

- Sit together and compare the playlists you created in the workbook. Compile your choices into an actual playlist and tell each other why you chose each specific song. If you have a favorite song together from your wedding or that has special meaning, take a few minutes to listen to it together.

- Go through the questions and exercises in the workbook, asking each other about how to best communicate. Be eager to listen. Don't be critical but be honest about what is most meaningful to you and lets you know that you're being understood and that you're loved.

- Read the words of Jesus and the proverb, sharing how each of those verses helped you think about healthy communication.

- Ask each other about any of the other things you read and wrote about in the *On Your Own* section on the previous pages. Remember, this is a conversation with your wife. Enjoy it!

- Go to *Love That Lasts* in your library at *bethkeworkshops.com* and watch this week's video: Communication with Jeff and Shaunti Feldhahn. They are experts in the field of relational communication and have a particular gift for using data and analysis to help us all better communicate. After watching, ask each other what was most interesting, most challenging, and a big takeaway from the video. Use the video sidebar to take notes and to help your conversation.

- Pray together.

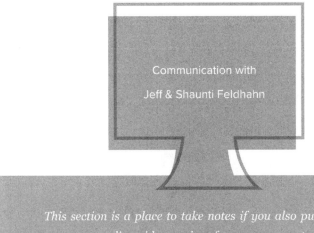

Communication with

Jeff & Shaunti Feldhahn

This section is a place to take notes if you also purchased the 12 corresponding video sessions from our 12 mentors. What did they say that resonated with you? What was your favorite part? What was most challenging?

_____

_____

_____

_____

_____

_____

_____

_____

_____

_____

_____

_____

_____

_____

_____

_____

_____

_____

_____

_____

_____

_____

_____

_____

_____

_____

_____

_____

_____

_____

_____

_____

_____

The one who guards his
mouth and tongue keeps
himself out of trouble.
Proverbs 21:23 (CSB)

If you don't have this video
you can purchase it at

lovethatlasts.co/videoseries

Conflict

04

Most couples, when asked, would probably say conflict is bad in a marriage. But I think we throw the baby out with the bathwater. Conflict is *inevitable* in a marriage. Two totally separate lives, two totally different personalities, and two different ways of doing things come crashing together in the marriage covenant. The issue isn't how do we eliminate conflict in our marriage; the issue is how do we eliminate *damaging* conflict in our marriage. Or to put it another way: there's a right way to fight in marriage, and there's a wrong way. Both are no fun, but in healthy conflict, with the proper tools, you aren't left hurt, confused, and divided. In fact, healthy conflict actually grows the couple in a substantial way over the long haul.

Alyssa and I have come to learn that when two people are involved in communication that means there are two different personalities at work, and, therefore, two different ways to communicate.

I love to process things out loud all the way to the end in the moment. Alyssa needs time to think about an issue by herself for a few hours or days to really feel ready to talk about it.

I am analytical and need logic and reasons to go down a certain path. Alyssa is sensitive and has "gut feelings" she sometimes can't explain to go down a certain path.

And in the beginning, because of our differences, we would sometimes have an inherent attitude that the way we were wired was the right way and the other person needed to change.

It's taken us a few years, but we now realize this is actually a blessing. Being opposite in decision making makes us a more well rounded couple. We are analytical and sensitive; we are rational and have gut feelings. It actually is God's blessing to us to make us better together.

One thing we've had to learn is to respect each other's way of communicating. So for Alyssa, she knows I like to really finish conversations, so it's not burdening me all day, so she tries hard to stay in it. But for me, I know if she's getting to the point where she can't make a decision in the moment, then I need to give her time and space to sit on it.

This is even truer in times when we start to get frustrated or upset. I've had to learn that even if I don't want to delay the conversation for a few more days (because I can't think about anything else except that, so it's not fun to delay it for me), it will serve us way better as a couple. When we realize our emotions are getting a little hotter and feelings are starting to get hurt, we call a time out. As author Anne Lamott expaied, "Almost everything will work again if you unplug it for a few minutes, including you." So we call for a break or a reset. Sometimes we even use a code word that means everything freezes. No more. We need space to think, calm down, pray, process, etc.

And guess what? When we do that, something magical happens. We come back calmer. We come back with more peace. We come back with changed hearts.

So commit as a couple today to set rules and boundaries for *how* you communicate during conflict. Agree to take breaks if things start escalating. Or make a code word. But most of all, understand that both personalities are a blessing when brought together and meant to make both people better

Write a powerful quote, song lyric, or Bible verse related to conflict. Draw a picture depicting the essence of conflict. You may want to journal your thoughts on a significant conflict that is burdening you of the effects of unresolved conflict in general.

GUIDEBOOK

Conflict

04

THEN PETER CAME TO HIM AND ASKED, "LORD, HOW OFTEN SHOULD I FORGIVE SOMEONE WHO SINS AGAINST ME? SEVEN TIMES?"

"NO, NOT SEVEN TIMES," JESUS REPLIED, "BUT SEVENTY TIMES SEVEN!"

Matthew 18:21-22 (NLT)

Conflict is inevitable. Let's just get the obvious out of the way. It's going to happen. Just like trust is built on little things and big things, conflict is going to happen in little things and big things. Let's commit to learning how to deal with conflict in the little things so that it doesn't escalate into something bigger. And whether we like to admit it or not, there will be times when we face more significant disagreements in marriage.

You may think that in a perfect world, we'd all just get along, but think about it: You saw the first husband and wife, Adam and Eve, blame each other for their disobedience to God in Genesis 3. Then you see their kids get into such a fight that one literally kills the other in Genesis 4. If Adam and Eve had conflict in a perfect world, then you and your wife and family members are going to have conflict. Until the new heaven and earth, where there will be no more pain, injustice, and death, we have to learn how to learn how to navigate conflict in a godly way.

In the Gospel of Matthew, Jesus' disciples asked him how to handle broken relationships. When people hurt us, how many chances do we give them before we walk away? How long should we put up with stubborn and selfish people? When do we say, *Enough is enough?*

Peter probably thought that his seven chances for serious offenses were generous. Symbolically, seven was a holy number of completion. Forgiving someone seven times may not have been a literal limit, but even if it was, the question for a specific could lead to a rigid and legalistic view of relationships. You can't plug relationships into a formula. There's no one-size-fits-all fit for everyone.

Jesus then says to take what we think would be godly and generous and then multiply that number exponentially. If seven times feels extremely gracious, multiply seven by another seven and then add a zero!

(Please note that forgiveness does not mean staying in an abusive or unhealthy situation. In that case, get help! The point is to focus on your own heart of forgiveness rather than on another person's actions.)

Even if we're on board with the whole forgiving thing, dealing with conflict in the first place may be difficult. We still need to learn to navigate the inevitably rough waters in order to make the journey as smooth as possible as a couple, as a family, as church members, as good neighbors, and in general as a human being in this world.

First, deal with conflict right away. Now, if you need to calm down for a minute, don't mistake this advice for saying something you'll regret by blowing up, but take a step back, catch your breath, and talk about whatever has upset you. You may actually be surprised at how many times what you're getting mad about is a misunderstanding and breakdown in communication.

But even if it leads to a tough conversation or an argument, the first step in learning to handle conflict is to stop putting things off and pretending like they don't bother you. You aren't helping anyone if you allow anger and unforgiveness to build up over time. Even if the conflict and offenses aren't big, the more you start to collect and the longer you carry them, the more they'll weigh you down and rob you of a joy and freedom as you walk with people through the days, weeks, months, and years. Even one tiny little pebble, when it gets in your shoe, can grow from an irritation to a serious problem. If you've ever gone to the beach, then you know that a tiny bit of sand in your shorts can ruin a great day if you don't shake it out!

One of the most practical verses in the Bible as far as conflict and healthy relationships is Ephesians 4:26: "Do not let the sun go down while you are still angry" (NIV). Like the "seventy times seven" verse, this may be figurative or it may be literal. When possible, it's a great practice in your marriage to take this at face value and promise your wife that the two of you will never end the day fighting with unresolved conflict. Don't get in bed with your backs turned in anger. Don't settle for the habit of storming out and refusing to sleep in the same room. This communicates an unwillingness to be joined together as one. In general, seek a resolution as soon as possible.

How many days last week did you literally go to sleep with something seriously bothering you?

1 · 2 · 3 · 4 · 5 · 6 · 7

Would any of those things fall into the "angry about it" category   **YES | NO**

If you can identify specific things that have upset you recently and are still unresolved, write them down here.

_____

_____

_____

_____

_____

_____

Pay attention this week to the things that upset you and how you dealt with it.

MY WEEK		
SUNDAY	**MONDAY**	**TUESDAY**
1	2	3

WEDNESDAY	**THURSDAY**	**FRIDAY**	**SATURDAY**
4	5	6	7

If you don't learn to deal with things quickly, you're choosing to allow conflict to pile up like rocks over what the Bible calls a *root of bitterness.* Since the beginning of time, our job has been to garden, to cultivate, and to flourish. The surest way to poison a relationship, including your marriage, is to slowly neglect a root of bitterness that needs to be pulled.

But don't just deal with them quickly; deal with them proportionately. Not all issues are the same. They all need dealt with, but not in the same way. Remember to address little things in little ways and big things in big ways.

You don't need to draw a line in the sand over how to load the dishwasher. You don't need to lose sleep coming to a resolution over how your shirts are folded or maybe not even always over how a careless word was more hurtful than intended. Mention it. Talk about it. But don't blow it out of proportion.

But sometimes there's a conflict that is really upsetting or where you are clearly on two opposite sides of an issue, like how to educate your kids or whether or not you'll even have kids, or what kind of home you'll move into, or how much travel is ok with your job. Sometimes the careless words or a pattern of thoughtlessness is worth losing sleep over so that the sun doesn't go down on what has become true hurt or anger.

A gentle answer turns away wrath, but a harsh word stirs up anger.

Proverbs 15:1 (NIV)

Write down a pet peeve or a personal preference that causes small degrees of tension (even if the conflict remains bottled up and never expressed).

_____

_____

_____

On a scale of 1 to 10, 1 = personal preference, 10 = I seriously can't live like this, how would you rate the issue?

1 · 2 · 3 · 4 · 5 · 6 · 7

YES | NO

Think about conflicts of various sizes. Is your reaction and method of addressing the issue typically proportional to its severity?

Circle your answer: I tend to: **OVERREACT | UNDERREACT**

Why do you sometimes overreact, exaggerating or fixating on conflict?

_____

_____

_____

Why do you sometimes underreact, minimizing or denying conflict?

_____

_____

_____

_____

_____

Right after the Bible says not to let the sun go down on your anger, it continues with "and do not give the devil a foothold" (Ephesians 4:27 NIV). Conflict that you don't shake out and put down become footholds for bitterness, doubt, jealousy, and all kinds of sin that calluses your heart until it is hardened toward that person—and eventually toward others too.

Eugene Peterson does a beautiful job in *The Message* of summarizing Jesus' teaching on addressing problems from Matthew 18:15-17: "If a fellow believer hurts you, go and tell him—work it out between the two of you. If he listens, you've made a friend. If he won't listen, take one or two others along so that the presence of witnesses will keep things honest, and try again. If he still won't listen, tell the church. If he won't listen to the church, you'll have to start over from scratch, confront him with the need for repentance, and offer again God's forgiving love."

This is commonly referred to as a Christian model of conflict resolution or of church discipline. Specifically, Jesus is addressing how to confront sin, but the pattern of conflict resolution applies:

1. One on one

2. With trusted friends

3. Get help from your church

4. Repeat

Here's the summary:

- If there's something that's bothering you, talk about it. Don't let it fester. Do it quickly but proportionately.

- If it bothers you to the point of being angry about it, don't go to sleep angry. Talk about it as soon as possible in an effort to find a grace-filled understanding.

- Talk one-on-one first. In your marriage, go straight to your wife, not to your friends. Keep in mind the principles of trust and communication. You love each other. Be humble. Assume the best. Desire understanding. Give grace.

- If something is a major problem, seek the counsel of a few trusted friends. But don't skip straight to this step. Develop a habit of talking one-on-one first.

- If you've been talking to each other and you've sought the counsel of trusted friends, but you still can't seem to find a healthy resolution, seek out the help of your church—pastors, counselors, or specialized ministries.

God designed you for relationships. Conflict is inevitable, but when you develop a habit of honest and humble communication out of a desire to love one another well, you'll cast of a huge burden and experience the joy of loving and forgiving, being loved and being forgiven, growing and flourishing together. For better and for worse and for better again.

JOIN
TOGETHER

Remember to give all of your attention to each other. Turn off or put down your phones. Don't miss this week's video. It's 20 minutes of expert advice in the truest sense of the word. It's literally sitting down in the kitchen with Drs. Les and Leslie Parrott, both who are bestselling psychologists and marriage counselors. Imagine what their conversations and arguments must be like!

By the way, Drs. Les and Leslie Parrott are the brilliant couple who put together the assessment you did as a couple. So you are already more familiar with their insightful ministry than you may have realized.

The *On Your Own* section was a little bit longer this time. Conflict by definition is harder to talk about, so enter this time joyfully and prayerfully.

- Sit together and pray, thanking God for His love for you and for the love you share for one another as a couple.
- Ask the following questions:

  → What are some little things we did differently and had to learn how to compromise and how to talk about those differences when we got married?

  → What funny quirks do I have that are part of who I am?

  → What habits or tendencies of mine have we learned to talk about as being unhelpful or hurtful?

  → When have we had to deal with a serious conflict with one another? It if escalated to a fight, what led to fighting and how have we learned from it?

  → When have we had to help one another deal with conflict outside of our marriage? For example, a bad work situation, trouble with a neighbor, or extended family drama. What steps did you take and what was the outcome? Do you think you dealt with it the right way?

- Read the words of Jesus and the proverb, sharing how each of those verses helped you think about a healthy perspective on conflict resolution.

- Ask each other about any of the other things you read and wrote about in the *On Your Own* section on the previous pages. Remember, this is a *conversation* with your wife, not a list of problems. The goal is to identify ways you can love and serve one another, recognizing potential conflict and learning how to address them early and lovingly so things don't escalate into fights or bitterness. The goal is seriousness but the conversation shouldn't necessarily be heavy.

  → Compare your thoughts and examples on the scale of *little* and *big* things. Did you have similar perspectives? Were there any major differences between what you consider a little or big deal?

  → Look at the calendar you kept and talk honestly about things you wrestled with this week. How can you help one another in those areas specifically?

  → Commit to the steps summarized at the end of the *On Your Own* portion of the section: deal immediately and proportionately, don't go to sleep angry, talk one-on-one first, then seek trusted counsel, finally seek help from your church pastors and ministries if a conflict ever gets to that point.

- Go to *Love That Lasts* in your library at *bethkeworkshops.com* and watch this week's video: Conflict with Les and Leslie Parrott. Then, ask each other what was most interesting, most challenging, and a big takeaway from the video. Use the video sidebar to take notes and to help your conversation.

- Pray together.

Conflict with

Les & Leslie Parrott

This section is a place to take notes if you also purchased the 12 corresponding video sessions from our 12 mentors. What did they say that resonated with you? What was your favorite part? What was most challenging?

If you don't have this video
you can purchase it at

lovethatlasts.co/videoseries

Faith

5

When I first met Alyssa, I remember being completely in awe. She was full of such grace and truth and carried herself in a way that she just glowed.

I'm not the only one who describes her like that. One of the things most people realize immediately is how much Alyssa radiates her love for Jesus. Every morning I can find her with coffee in her hand and a Bible in her lap, reading and praying.

This is actually one of the things that most attracted me to her. I knew I wanted to be in a marriage where faith was held in high regards because a solid faith builds a solid marriage. Faith is the rock to stand on when the marriage faces difficulties, hard seasons, infertility, a loss of someone close, distance, and on and on. Faith is what carries us through.

But how do we actually put this into practice? How do we talk about the things of God together? What about a plan to read the Bible together? It all sounds like a good idea, but the practicality of actually living in a way where each other's faith is sharpening the other, takes time and effort.

Building a marriage on faith comes down to knowing your personalities. For example, I love to read. A lot. My faith is strengthened by reading books and internally processing. Alyssa though is a lot more relational. She is usually most encouraged by deep heart-to-heart talks with friends, me, or when we have other married couples over for dinner.

It's important to know this about each other because we want to be in a marriage where both of us are always feeling filled up, encouraged, and sharpened. This means I usually need some alone time, and it also means I have to be sensitive to Alyssa's needs and always checking in on her heart. When I do this poorly, it usually means a couple days have gone by and Alyssa and I haven't had a serious and deep conversation. Sometimes it's only 10 minutes, but if it's intentional and thoughtful and deep, that matters to her.

Something funny happens in those moments when I'm trying to be thoughtful toward Alyssa. It encourages and strengthens me too. There's something about building up someone else's faith and looking to serve them that builds up your own faith. It's like a mutual cycle and dance that continually builds off each other.

But the question still remains, how do you do it? Alyssa and I work on the following:

1. Pray for each other. This is the highest calling you have as a husband. Praying for your wife is one of the best things you can do. Lift up her passions, dreams, and desires. Ask the Lord to bless her. Pray for her when she's down. Pray for her when she's up. Prayer is the lifeline of a marriage, and when taken advantage of, something special happens. It changes not only your spouse, but yourself. It softens your heart, creates more patience and compassion in you too.

2. Shepherd one another's hearts. This will look differently for each couple. Regardless of how it looks though, we are called to encourage and speak truth into each other's lives. Share what God is teaching you, what you're reading or listening to, and talk about scripture and sermons and values. Ask her how his heart is, what she's been thinking about lately, what's weighing her down, how you can pray and serve her.

3. What is God calling you to as a couple or family? What gifts and callings and passions do you all have? How can you make God known, and be his hands and feet, together as a couple? Do you love babies and want to serve in the nursery at church together? Do you want to open your home to foster care or those without father figures? Do you want to start a Bible study together or mentor a younger couple? Do you want to hand out lunches to the homeless once a month or disciple high schoolers? What can you do together? Because marriage doesn't end with us; it's about being on mission together and that brings the most joy.

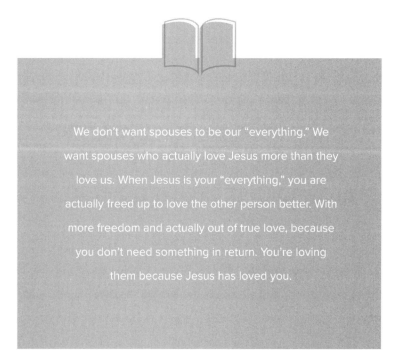

We don't want spouses to be our "everything." We want spouses who actually love Jesus more than they love us. When Jesus is your "everything," you are actually freed up to love the other person better. With more freedom and actually out of true love, because you don't need something in return. You're loving them because Jesus has loved you.

GUIDEBOOK

Faith

"TEACHER, WHICH
COMMAND IN THE LAW
IS THE GREATEST?"
[JESUS] SAID TO HIM,
"LOVE THE LORD
YOUR GOD WITH ALL
YOUR HEART, WITH
ALL YOUR SOUL, AND
WITH ALL YOUR MIND.
THIS IS THE GREATEST
AND MOST IMPORTANT
COMMAND. THE
SECOND IS LIKE IT:
LOVE YOUR NEIGHBOR
AS YOURSELF. ALL
THE LAW AND THE
PROPHETS DEPEND
ON THESE TWO
COMMANDS."

Matthew 22:36-40 (CSB)

Jesus said that God's will for our entire lives could be summed up in loving God above anything or anyone else, and then loving others as if their needs were your own. This summarizes the Christian faith. He said that everything written in the Old Testament—all the rules, instructions, prophetic corrections and promises—all of it ultimately boils down to truly loving God and loving one another.

It's that simple, but we know our own hearts and that the simplicity doesn't mean it's easy. In fact, as you've been digging into these last topics of trust, communication, and conflict, relationships are hard work. There's nothing more satisfying than a right relationship with God and with others, especially in marriage, but there's nothing that requires more intentionality.

In his book *For the Love,* D. A. Carson put our need for intentionality this way: "People do not drift toward holiness." Think about how true that is in your own experience. He goes on to explain: "Apart from grace-driven effort, people do not gravitate toward godliness, prayer, obedience to Scripture, faith, and delight in the Lord."

Living near the beach, it's easy to see the tides change and the rhythms in nature. But you don't have to stand on the shore to see this simple truth. Look up at the sky. Even on a still day, if you watch long enough, you begin to see the slow movement and changing shapes of the clouds as they drift through the sky.

Everything is moving. The question for you is whether or not you are moving closer to God, growing deeper in your faith, or are you drifting away from Him. If you aren't paying attention or intentionally focusing your heart on God, then you will be pushed along by the changing tides and shifting winds of each day. You'll drift away.

This reality of naturally drifting away and never drifting toward is true in your love for God and for one another in marriage (or any relationship). Jesus is clear that when your love for God is a priority, then your relationships can take their rightful place and shape. When our love for God and for one another is pure, then we'll find that Scripture and all that it reveals about abundant and eternal life finds new clarity and meaning. Faith moves from our heads, to our hearts, spilling out into our relationships and into everything we do.

What things do you naturally find yourself drifting toward—what consumes your thoughts, emotions, motivations, and activities?

_____

_____

_____

_____

When do you feel your thoughts, feelings, and activities most prone to drift away from faith in God?

_____

_____

_____

Think about the specific language used to describe the ways you should love God and people.

What does it mean and what does it look like to *love the Lord your God with all your heart, with all your soul, and with all your mind?*

_____

_____

_____

_____

What does it mean and what does it look like to *love your neighbor as yourself?*

_____

_____

_____

As water reflects the face,

so one's life reflects the heart.

Proverbs 27:19

Write a favorite quote, song lyric, or Bible verse related to faith or belief. Draw a picture of a vine. Write about the first time you began to understand what faith in God truly meant.

ON YOUR OWN

Jesus uses a beautiful picture of this organic connection in our relationships with God and with each other. Look at how he explained faith and love to his disciples.

> I am the vine; you are the branches. The one who remains in me and I in him produces much fruit, because you can do nothing without me.
>
> As the Father has loved me, I have also loved you. Remain in my love. If you keep my commands you will remain in my love, just as I have kept my Father's commands and remain in his love.
>
> I have told you these things so that my joy may be in you and your joy may be complete. This is my command: Love one another as I have loved you.
>
> John 15:5, 9-12 (CSB)

The disciple who wrote down these words, John, was practically obsessed with love. It was a healthy obsession. In fact, he refers to himself in his Gospel as "the disciple Jesus loved." This wasn't an arrogant nickname, suggesting that Jesus loved him more than the other disciples. It's a testimony to the reality that John's life was so transformed by his relationship with Jesus that his entire identity could be summed up by the fact that Jesus loved him.

In the verses you just read, Jesus is teaching his disciples that every good thing in their life will grow out of their relationship with God. Their lives are to be defined by love for God and for one another. Literally nothing that is truly good is possible apart from his blessings. God is good. God is love. Loving God and loving one another are inseparable; you can't do one without the other (1 John 4:8). A vine is the source of life for branches. Branches can't live and bear fruit without the vine. Jesus is saying that it's impossible to experience abundant life, joy, satisfaction, and true love without being deeply rooted in and dependent on God's love to flow through you.

Faith in God means trusting that he is everything we need for joy and satisfaction in life. Obedience to God is an act of love. It's a way of saying, "I believe that you always know what is best for me." God's commands are an expression of his love for his children. Your heavenly Father loves you. Jesus loves you. What could possibly be better than that? Let this

	SUNDAY	MONDAY	TUESDAY
	1	2	3
YOU			
YOUR WIFE			

truth change your life so completely that it flows into your relationships, bearing good fruit for the whole world to "taste and see that the Lord is good" (Psalm 34:8).

We'll look at several different rhythms in life that focus our hearts on the love of God later in this workbook, so for now let's start with the simple definition of faith of loving God and loving one another, using the points that were introduced in reading.

Pray for your wife.

Write down a specific topic of prayer each day this week related to how you want God to draw you and your wife deeper into relationship with him.

WEDNESDAY	THURSDAY	FRIDAY	SATURDAY
4	5	6	7

Shepherd one another's hearts.

What is God teaching you right now that you can share with your wife?

_____

_____

_____

_____

How can you encourage or help your wife with Christlike love?

_____

_____

_____

_____

How can she encourage you?

_____

_____

_____

What is God calling you to as a couple, or family?

_____

_____

_____

What opportunities do you have to encourage other people—neighbors, coworkers, friends, church, community—to grow in their faith?

_____

_____

_____

How are you involved in your church, connected to other branches in the vine?

_____

_____

_____

If you're not currently involved in a church, what church would you like to visit?

_____

_____

_____

JOIN
TOGETHER

Remember to give all of your attention to each other. Turn off or put down your phones. This week's video is the shortest in the series, only 15 minutes, but it is packed with wisdom from an incredible couple talking about faith in God and God's faithfulness to us.

(Side note: One of the ways that the church pastored by one of this week's featured video mentors seeks to help people grow in their faith is with The Bible App and The Bible App for Kids by YouVersion.)

- Sit together and pray, thanking God for His love for you and for the love you share for one another as a couple.
- If you did the creative option of a quote, picture, or journal, share that with each other.
- Read the words of Jesus and the proverb, sharing how each of those verses helped you think about your faith.
- Ask each other about any of the other things you read and wrote about in the *On Your Own* section on the previous pages.
- Go to *Love That Lasts* in your library at *bethkeworkshops.com* and watch this week's video: Faith with Craig and Amy Groeschel. Then, ask each other what was most interesting, most challenging, and a big takeaway from the video. Use the video sidebar to take notes and to help your conversation.

Faith with

Craig & Amy Groeschel

This section is a place to take notes if you also purchased the 12 corresponding video sessions from our 12 mentors. What did they say that resonated with you? What was your favorite part? What was most challenging?

_____

_____

_____

_____

_____

_____

_____

_____

_____

_____

_____

_____

_____

_____

If you don't have this video
you can purchase it at

lovethatlasts.co/videoseries

Calling and
Purpose

06

One of the biggest things any marriage has to walk through is the coming together of two dreams, two passions, and two giftings. And in that collision there's a lot to figure out. How do we do both? Does one win or lose? Does one take the backseat while the other gets to live their calling?

This is at least how I thought about it for the longest time. In our marriage, we generally felt called to the same things, which made life on this issue pretty simple. We both saw ourselves writing, pouring into other people our age or younger, in person or on the internet, and making videos and resources for them. And so we did that for the first couple years, and it was a blast.

But there was one place of tension that always came up time and time again—traveling and speaking. I have always loved it, and living out of suitcases doesn't bother me one bit. For Alyssa though it's draining and feels like an eternal limbo. But the fact we were travelling together and adventuring all over the globe was still fun for her. We have been to Uganda, Germany, London, Italy, and probably over 25 to 30 states together. It was a blast and such a fun way to go through our first couple years of marriage.

Then we had kids.

And I still wanted to travel and try to do it as a family, but it was even more grueling for Alyssa than it was before kids. Now it meant infants and toddlers traveling over time zones and planning feedings and nap schedules while on an airplane.

But I kept coming back to the fact that I felt "called" to speaking and preaching and so even though it was hard, we'd have to still try as a family. What it turned into was sometimes the family would come, and sometimes they wouldn't. If they came, it was hard. And if they didn't, it was hard. I started to feel a check in my spirit about it but kept falling back on the fact this was right in my wheelhouse of gifting and calling. So how could we not do it?

Then I had a conversation with some of our closest mentors that completely rocked my world. I remember him saying, "Jeff, you're not single anymore. Your calling and gifting is no longer just *your* calling and gifting. God doesn't work like that. He gives the unit a calling. So if it's a husband and wife, then He gives them together as a couple a gifting or calling or space out in the marketplace. And if they have kids, then He calls the family to something, not just the dad or the mom. So if other people in the family are sinking at the expense of 'your calling,' then it actually probably isn't."

We immediately changed everything and couldn't be happier. It was clear from the first day that his words were true. God didn't give someone a calling, and then make the whole family suffer to serve that calling. That's not how it works. He calls a married couple or a family. And of course people have different giftings and talents and jobs but it has to be serving the marriage or the family well, or it's probably not the best fit.

Write a favorite quote, song lyric, or Bible verse related to purpose. For this week's artistic option, draw either something to represent what you believe to be your ultimate purpose, what the next step of faith may be, or how you feel trying to figure out God's purpose for your life.

Calling and Purpose

AS JESUS
WALKED BESIDE
THE SEA OF
GALILEE, HE SAW
SIMON AND HIS
BROTHER ANDREW
CASTING
A NET INTO
THE LAKE, FOR
THEY WERE
FISHERMEN.
"COME, FOLLOW
ME," JESUS SAID,
"AND I WILL SEND
YOU OUT TO FISH
FOR PEOPLE." AT
ONCE THEY LEFT
THEIR NETS AND
FOLLOWED HIM.

Mark 1:16-18 (NIV)

Simon and Andrew weren't just spending a weekend on the lake, fishing with their buddies. Fishing was the family business, their career. Then Jesus completely turned their world upside down and gave them a brand new purpose and meaning to what they already knew how to do. Jesus spoke to them in a way that they understood and called them in the middle of their normal, everyday life. Immediately Simon and Andrew dropped what they were doing in order to experience what Jesus had in store for their lives.

The same was true for James and John whom Jesus would call in the next verses—the same John who wrote the famous Gospel of John, 1-3 John, and the Book of Revelation! Those books are possibly the most beautiful and awe-inspiring literature in the New Testament.

There are a few of things to notice in these verses:

- When Jesus called them, He didn't give them all of the details.
- Even though they weren't expecting it, they followed His calling immediately, believing that He was worth any change of plans or personal sacrifice.
- Jesus' purpose for their lives expanded on what they already knew and were good at, but He did something that they never would have imagined.

These three things are true about God's purpose for your life too. He is calling you into relationship with Him and there is absolutely no way to know exactly what all He has in store for you as you follow Him in faith. But you can know for sure that it will be worth it.

Here's something else to consider: Simon and Andrew, James and John, and any of the other disciples may not have even realized when they dropped those nets that this was the first step of faith that would change the rest of their lives. Chances are, they didn't understand in that moment that they would have to make some decisions about the fishing business and how it fit into their lives as followers of Jesus. They just knew that in that moment, they wanted to follow him. And the next day they would essentially make that decision again. And again. And again. And three years later, as Jesus was hanging on a cross, they didn't fully understand what was happening. Surely their minds raced back to all of the decisions they had made and the conversations they had with family and friends and coworkers, explaining that they were going to follow Jesus.

Had they been crazy? Did they make a terrible decision? Did they completely misunderstand what Jesus wanted them to do?

After Jesus was resurrected, the disciples were found fishing (see John 21). Jesus is once again standing on the beach calling out to His disciples, asking about the day's catch. When Simon Peter realizes that it's Jesus, he dives in the water, fully clothed, and swims back to Jesus. John and the other disciples row back and meet him. It's actually pretty comical. But the Bible shows us over and over that God calls ordinary people for his extraordinary purpose.

While everyone won't be called to leave their professions in order to go into "career ministry" jobs, God's purpose for each of our lives is to follow Jesus. This is ultimately an application of what it means to "love God and love people" in your own life and sphere of influence. As Colossians 3:17 puts it, "Whatever you do, in word or deed, do everything in the name of the Lord Jesus, giving thanks to God the Father through him" (ESV).

1. How would you define the purpose of life in general?

_____

_____

_____

_____

_____

_____

2. What would you say is your purpose in life as a follower of Jesus?

_____

_____

_____

_____

_____

_____

3. What are your specific talents and God-given abilities?

_____

_____

_____

_____

_____

_____

4. How would you describe your personality?

_____

_____

_____

_____

_____

5. What are your interests, hobbies, and passions?

_____

_____

_____

_____

_____

6. If you could do anything in the world with your life, what would it be?

_____

_____

_____

_____

_____

_____

7. What experiences in your past have shaped who you are today?

_____

_____

_____

_____

_____

8. How do those things identified above fit into current opportunities?

_____

_____

_____

_____

_____

9. What would it look like to use your abilities, passions, dreams, and opportunities to better love God, to love others, and to help others enter into and grow in a relationship with Jesus?

_____

_____

_____

_____

_____

_____

10. What are your wife's natural abilities and unique gifts?

_____

_____

_____

_____

_____

11. How would you describe her personality?

_____

_____

_____

_____

_____

12. What are her interests, hobbies, and passions?

_____

_____

_____

_____

_____

13. If she could do anything in the world with her life, what do you think it would be?

_____

_____

_____

_____

14. What experiences in her past have shaped who she is today?

_____

_____

_____

_____

_____

15. How have you seen God working in her and through her?

_____

_____

_____

_____

_____

16. What is something special about how she shows the love of Christ to people that she may not know about herself?

_____

_____

_____

_____

17. When you consider all of these things about your life and about hers, what might God want to do through your life together?

_____

_____

_____

_____

_____

18. How can you encourage her in her unique opportunities?

_____

_____

_____

_____

_____

19. How can she encourage you in your unique opportunities?

_____

_____

_____

_____

_____

20. Even if you don't know what you're called to when it comes to some big special purpose, what step of faith can you take as a couple or as a family to experience God and to share His love with others?

_____

_____

_____

_____

JOIN
TOGETHER

Remember to give all of your attention to each other. Turn off or put down your phones. This week may take more time to discuss the questions, Scriptures, and video, so be sure to plan accordingly. The video is only 20 minutes and it's a fantastic resource on how two unique callings in life can work together in a beautiful way as a couple.

- Sit together and pray, thanking God that He has a plan for your lives as individuals and as a couple or family. Ask God to begin making his purpose for your lives clear and to give you the confidence to step out in faith, one step at a time.

- If you did the creative option of a quote, picture, or journal, share that with each other.

- Read the words of Jesus and the proverb, sharing how each of those verses helped you think about your faith.

- Walk through each of the 20 questions you did on your own, comparing your answers. Don't stress. It's not about quizzing each other to get the right answers. This is an awesome way to get to know your wife in a deeper and more intimate way.

- Note: Your questions 1-9 will line up with her 10-19. Question 20 is your answer as a couple.

- Go to *Love That Lasts* in your library at *bethkeworkshops.com* and watch this week's video: Purpose with Zac and Jennie Allen. Then, ask each other what was most interesting, most challenging, and a big takeaway from the video. Use the video sidebar to take notes and to help your conversation. ▣

Purpose with

Zac & Jennie Allen

This section is a place to take notes if you also purchased the 12 corresponding video sessions from our 12 mentors. What did they say that resonated with you? What was your favorite part? What was most challenging?

_____

_____

_____

_____

_____

_____

_____

_____

_____

_____

_____

_____

_____

Trust in the Lord with all your
heart and lean not on your
own understanding; in all your
ways submit to him, and he
will make your paths straight.
Proverbs 3:5-6 (NIV)

If you don't have this video
you can purchase it at

lovethatlasts.co/videoseries

Sex

7

Sex is a tricky thing. It's usually one of those things we learn about wrongly first, and then try to undo years of baggage and harmful teaching, in hopes of coming around to a healthy view of sex and marriage.

At least that's my story.

I first saw porn in my tween years and became fully addicted by age 13 or 14. I started dating and getting into unhealthy relationships at 16, which lasted all the way until my freshman year of college.

So when I started to walk with Jesus, and then try to attempt to date and pursue a relationship in a healthy way, it took some intense work. I had serious baggage and serious healing to do, specifically in the realm of sex.

One of my main obstacles was I was trained by pornography, my friends, and MTV that sex was primarily about self gratification and taking. It was about me and using another person to get what I want. And it was through me opening up the scriptures in a new way at age 19 that I started to see that was never God's intention at all.

Yes, sex was meant to feel good. But using it for taking and self-gratification was cheap pleasure. Kind of like a 30-year-old man swimming in the kiddie pool. Sure, it might feel good on a hot day. But he looks stupid, and he was created for the deep end of the pool. *There's so much more.*

And that's the picture we see in scripture. Sex is actually two bodies coming together and making true in their bodies what they are making true in their lives. Sex is a picture of the marriage covenant. It's saying I give myself to you fully, vulnerably, lovingly everyday for the rest of my life.

But sadly, sex doesn't always seem that good or that picture doesn't play out in most marriages. There are unmet expectations. Hurt feelings. Unhealed pasts. What do you do when even your spouse's touch makes you recoil? Or when kids and toddlers and cheerios have literally just made you forget since you fall asleep at 7:30pm now?

For Alyssa and I, it's been a journey. But that's the beauty of marriage. You have a lifetime together, and you get to take advantage of that journey. To learn each other's preferences. Each other's bodies. Each other's desires. And you get to serve one another, in mutual self-giving love.

So for us, even though we haven't been married long, here are two helpful things we've found that really seem to get to the heart of sex and create the intimacy that was meant to be created between a husband and wife.

1. Give, don't take. One of the things that's easy to lose sight of is that sex is about two people. And sadly our culture with all its objectification has trained us to think it's about what we can get out of it. But don't let that mindset in your marriage or your bedroom. Jesus said it's more blessed to give than receive. And that is true in sex too. For sex to be sex at the level it was created to be, it comes down to both spouses looking to serve the other, not take what they can. Continually cultivate that value in the bedroom, and you'll see just how beautiful it is.

2. Communicate. Alyssa and I both had enough church backgrounds in our upbringing to feel sometimes that the message was sex was dirty and don't talk about it. But the truth is, it's an amazing gift and talking is one of the best things you can do. Be honest. Ask questions of each other. What do you like? What do you not like? When do you most feel like having sex? When do you not? How can I serve you? And so on.

Remember, it's a picture of the covenant. I remember hearing pastor Tim Keller say that sex is pretty much just renewing your wedding vows. It's using your bodies as a picture of your vows. That you are each other's forever until death do you part. Also, Jeremy and Audrey Roloff (Beating50percent.com) suggest printing out your wedding vows and reading them to each other while you're having sex once a year. While it sounds awkward, it turns into one of the sweetest and most intimate moments in a marriage. A reminder of your love, your covenant, your promise. And sex is a picture of that.

You are fully loved and fully known. I think sex operates on the highest level it was meant to, when we realize it's an acceptance of the other amidst all their flaws, frailties, and imperfections. When someone sees all that you are, in full nakedness (bodily, emotionally, and mentally) and still says, "I see you and I want to be one with you" that is the essence of love. Being fully known and fully loved at the same time is the center of intimacy.

GUIDEBOOK
Sex

[JESUS] ANSWERED, "HAVEN'T YOU READ IN YOUR BIBLE THAT THE CREATOR ORIGINALLY MADE MAN AND WOMAN FOR EACH OTHER, MALE AND FEMALE? AND BECAUSE OF THIS, A MAN LEAVES FATHER AND MOTHER AND IS FIRMLY BONDED TO HIS WIFE, BECOMING ONE FLESH—NO LONGER TWO BODIES BUT ONE. BECAUSE GOD CREATED THIS ORGANIC UNION OF THE TWO SEXES, NO ONE SHOULD DESECRATE HIS ART BY CUTTING THEM APART."

Matthew 19:4-6 (MSG)

You're not having déjà vu. You read a different translation of these verses in the first session, *Theology of Marriage.* But it's important to catch something that may not be obvious, especially if you're familiar with the "two shall become one" language of marriage.

This may not exactly be the illustration you were hoping for in a chapter about sex, but stay with me. Imagine a debate or talk show where someone is trying to back someone else into a corner with a polarizing question that can only be answered in a way that offends one side of an issue or the other. Even worse, if the person tries to dodge the question by not answering it, he loses credibility with both sides. It's a lose-lose-lose situation. This is exactly what it was happening when the religious leaders of Jesus' day attempt to trap him with a question about whether or not it's ever okay to get a divorce.

Of course Jesus' answer is brilliant. He doesn't answer or avoid their question. He swings the spotlight back over onto his opponents, asking them whether or not they understand one of the most elementary yet profound truths in Scripture. This is *Bible 101: Introduction to God and Humankind.* Jesus basically says, "Before we talk about ending a marriage, let's be sure that everyone here understands the mind-blowingly beautiful miracle that God did with creation and continues to do in marriage. Did you guys somehow skip the first pages of your Bibles? You really should go back and read them. Seriously. It's fantastic stuff."

Eugene Peterson's paraphrase of the Bible does a beautiful job of highlighting the fact that spirituality and sexuality are intertwined in marriage. This is why God is so clear throughout Scripture that sex and marriage should be treasured as uniquely beautiful gifts. Sex in marriage is a masterpiece by our

Creator. Taking sex outside of its perfectly designed context, making it an act of the self rather than of union, or anything that desecrates the sacred marriage covenant is like taking scissors to a priceless work of art.

Look at these phrases describing marriage:

> *... made man and woman for each other ...*
> *... firmly bonded to his wife, becoming one flesh*
> *—no longer two bodies but one ...*
> *... this organic union of the two sexes ...*

Don't dismiss this language as purely symbolic and poetic. Yes, there is a theological and metaphorical significance to two becoming one, but it's also a very literal and sexual union of two bodies becoming one flesh—one man and one woman.

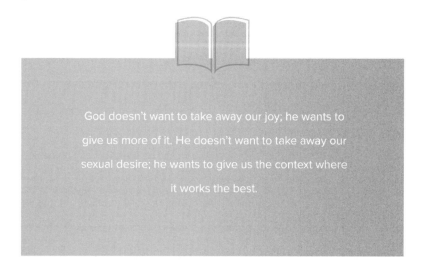

God doesn't want to take away our joy; he wants to give us more of it. He doesn't want to take away our sexual desire; he wants to give us the context where it works the best.

ON YOUR OWN

Sex was God's idea. It's a really good idea! Christians often have the mistaken belief that sex is taboo and dirty. This is not only a mistake, but it's a harmful distortion of this amazing gift. But for a long time, the Church found it easiest just to tell kids that it was bad and not do it until you get married and then it's good. Talk about whiplash!

Sin has hijacked one of God's greatest gifts. Sexual desire for and pleasure in your spouse has always been part of the way God made men and women.

When did you first learn about sex?

_____

_____

_____

What was your earliest understanding of sex?

_____

_____

_____

How did friends, family, and culture influence your view of sex?

_____

_____

_____

How did the Church, the Bible, or Christians influence your view of sex?

_____

_____

_____

Have you ever talked about any sexual background with your wife?

_____

_____

_____

Do you talk openly about sex with your wife now—what you like, what she likes, etc.?

_____

_____

_____

On a scale of 1-10 (1 = all about me, 10 = all about her) how would you rate your view of sex? (Not rating your view on how good sex is, but on whether or not your focus is honestly more on you or her.)

1 · 2 · 3 · 4 · 5 · 6 · 7 · 8 · 9 · 10

All about me   *All about her*

Look back at the verses Jesus was quoting earlier.

> *So the Lord God caused a deep sleep to come over the man, and he*
> *slept. God took one of his ribs and closed the flesh at that place. Then*
> *the Lord God made the rib he had taken from the man into a woman*
> *and brought her to the man. And the man said:*
> *This one, at last, is bone of my bone*
> *and flesh of my flesh;*
> *this one will be called "woman,"*
> *for she was taken from man.*
> *This is why a man leaves his father and mother and bonds with his*
> *wife, and they become one flesh. Both the man and his wife were*
> *naked, yet felt no shame.*
> *Genesis 2:21-25 (CSB)*

You see this picture of an intimate moment where God creates woman and presents her to the man. It's like a wedding where the bride is given to the groom. And look at the first thing Adam does when he sees Eve for the first time. He starts singing a love song! And the chapter closes as if the curtain was being drawn for the honeymoon as they were naked and felt no shame—only knowing the kind of joy that caused spontaneous singing.

That's the kind of sex and nakedness and intimacy between a husband and a wife that God has created for you. This doesn't necessarily mean that you should sing next time you see your wife, but you can certainly praise her and declare your love for and awe of her, thanking God for his kindness to you in blessing you with your marriage. Proverbs 31:31 talks about praising your wife at the city gates. Now you may want to go the 1980's route with the *Say Anything* boombox-over-the-head serenade, or you may want to do something ... not so 1980's.

Get creative and do something fun or romantic to surprise your wife. It doesn't have to be a crazy-elaborate gesture, it may be as simple as surprising her at work, leaving notes, or cooking a favorite meal.

Share a picture of you and your wife on instagram, facebook, twitter, or whatever your social media of choice happens to be. Thank God for your wife and expressing your love for her. We'd love to see these too, so if you want to spread the love with everyone else, don't forget to use the hashtag #LoveThatLasts.

Write a favorite quote, song lyric, or Bible verse related to desire for your wife. For this week's creative option, think about a song that is romantic or sexy. You may even want to add to the previous playlist you created or create a new playlist for your own mood music.

JOIN
TOGETHER

Remember to give all of your attention to each other. Turn off or put down your phones. Hopefully, giving each other attention should be extra enjoyable this week. In fact, you may want to plan for either a longer date night tonight or possibly split this up into two times together because the video this week is 45 minutes. Craig and Jeanette provide one of the most candid conversations about a healthy sex life. Seriously, when was the last time sex positions were discussed in a Bible study? But don't freak out (or get overly excited): it's not a how-to guide to Christian sex.

While it may not feel all that romantic to take notes, you're going to want to pay attention to their wisdom when it comes to expectations, communication, etc. The goal is to help you see sex clearly as God created it—and to fully enjoy one another!

- Sit together and pray, thanking God for the intimacy he has created you to share with one another—spiritually, emotionally, and sexually. Ask him to draw you closer to one another in every way and to bless your marriage.
- Read the words of Jesus and the proverb, sharing how each of those verses helped you think about sex.
- Ask and share about anything from anything else from the *On Your Own* section or the personal reading.
- Go to *Love That Lasts* in your library at *bethkeworkshops.com* and watch this week's video: Sex with Craig and Jeanette Gross. Then, ask each other what was most interesting, most challenging, and a big takeaway from the video. Use the video sidebar to take notes and to help your conversation.

- If this hasn't been a date night the past several times (or whatever time of the day you may be meeting), make it a special time. You may want to have some food or snacks and something to drink.
- Share memories from your wedding night and honeymoon. If you have pictures of the honeymoon, look at those together like you did with the wedding pictures during the first session.

  → What were you thinking and feeling that first night we were married?

  → What are your favorite memories from the honeymoon?

  → What were you most excited about? Nervous about?

  → Was anything surprising, or did anything funny happen?

  → Do you remember anything funny happening while having sex?

  → What are some of the best times you've had sex? What made those experiences especially good?

  → What do you not like? What do you really like? What would you like?

- If you did the creative option of choosing a song or making a playlist, play the music and tell your wife why you chose that first song. What about it makes you think of her?
- Take a break to express your love for one another. Show your wife that you care about her needs.

Sex with

Craig & Jeanette Gross

This section is a place to take notes if you also purchased the
12 corresponding video sessions from our 12 mentors. What did
they say that resonated with you? What was your favorite part?
What was most challenging?

_____

_____

_____

_____

_____

_____

_____

_____

_____

_____

_____

_____

_____

_____

_____

_____

_____

_____

_____

_____

_____

_____

_____

_____

_____

_____

_____

_____

_____

_____

_____

_____

_____

> Let your fountain be blessed, and rejoice in the wife of your youth, a lovely deer, a graceful doe. Let her breasts fill you at all times with delight; be intoxicated always in her love.
>
> Proverbs 5:18-19

If you don't have this video
you can purchase it at

lovethatlasts.co/videoseries

Parenting

8

When our oldest, Kinsley, was maybe 2 months old, I was laying on my back on the ground, holding her up above me and playing with her. She was smiling and laughing. Then all of a sudden I see this white stuff fall from her mouth.

Because I was laughing and smiling with her, my mouth was open. It falls right into my mouth.

That was the moment I really knew I was officially a parent, and there was no going back. Poopy diapers, spit up, old cheerios stuck in the car seat, were all things that are now very much a part of my life.

And I love every second of it.

Kids are such a blessing, and being a parent is hard. But it's a blessing too.

But one thing that a lot of people don't talk about, or something we didn't feel like there were a lot of resources on, was how to parent in a way that also supports and protects your marriage.

Because the truth is, a lot of times we get married, start having kids, and our marriage starts to take a hit. We are exhausted, we barely have time for naps let alone each other, and we seem to be more irritable than ever.

So how do you have a healthy vision for parenting that also uplifts and supports your marriage?

Alyssa and I have been blessed with some incredible mentors in this area, so I'll share a couple of the most helpful things we've learned so far.

1. Create culture. Because parenting is so hard and very much 0 to 60 in 2 seconds, a lot of us take the default position of reacting rather than acting. We are reactive instead of proactive. And that is a sure way to lead to exhausting and relational strife. Get out ahead of it by casting a vision for your family and your marriage. I'll never forget something some of our mentors said to us before we had kids. They said, "Make sure you set and create a culture in the home before you have kids. If not, they will set it." What he was saying was that it's very easy for the kids to set the rules and tones of the home if you don't already have a vision and culture in place. But he reminded me, "Jeff, remember that when you bring a kid home from the hospital, you are bringing them into an already built culture, marriage, and way of doing things." That mindset has been life-changing for us. It helps teach our kiddos they aren't the center, but rather we are all shooting for this vision and goal of a home that loves and serves Jesus well and each other well, and they are welcomed into that mission that we have already started. So whether you have kids or not, ask yourself what culture are you creating in the home. If someone had to describe your parenting style, what would it be? Do you like what they'd say? Be proactive, set some big picture values, and set a culture that allows your family and marriage to thrive.

2. Whatever you train to, you create. This is something Alyssa and I have to remind ourselves of every day. If you always give five warnings to your kids before you finally follow through, then most likely they will only start listening to you after five warnings. So this again goes to the above point, but train toward whatever culture you want to create. Do you want to have kids who listen right away? It's exceptionally hard, but work toward instructing them to listen on the first ask. So always be mindful of whatever you are training to, because that is most likely what will be created.

3. Always think big picture. This was helpful advice from our friends Korie and Willie Robertson. The little things are important (like throwing away our trash after you eat a granola bar), but the big things are more important (like being kind and generous) so give those things most of your time and energy as a parent. Don't get so exhausted by the little things that you have no energy left to instill kindness, creativity, critical thinking, gentleness, and love in them.

4. You are not a babysitter, you're a dad. Dads, please don't ever say you're "babysitting" the kids. You're not. You're being their father. I think one the hurtful pictures the older generations gave us as dads is that being a dad means working hard then coming home and sitting on the couch and watching football. But being a dad is a full-time job, and a full-time joy. We might work hard and/or are the primary source of income for our family (or maybe not), but before our jobs, we are called to be good husbands and fathers. To change diapers. Do the dishes. Check in on the kid's hearts. Play with them. Ask them good questions. Mow the lawn. Take them to practice. You and your wife are parenting as a team. It's not her primary job. It's both of your privilege.

5. Marriage first, kids second. At the end of the day it's helpful to remember, your kids will leave, but your marriage won't. So building it in such a way that your kids see your marriage is the center of the family. Creating a child-centered home can be destructive to not only the parents, but the kids too. Investing in your marriage will always be an investment in your kids, because nothing is a bigger blessing to our kids than to show them a marriage that loves each other, fights for each other, and are each other's number one fans and best friends.

Even though we don't realize it, having a loving and healthy marriage example in your parents has profound impact on you. Tens of thousands of micro moments and conversations and watching your mom and dad love and serve each other, amidst their problems and baggage, and all those other things, adds up over thousands of hours to show you what it takes. To show you what it looks like.

Write your favorite quote,
song lyric, or Bible verse
related to babies, kids, or
growing up. If you're extra
artistic, get creative with your
handwriting or draw something
to represent family.

GUIDEBOOK

Parenting

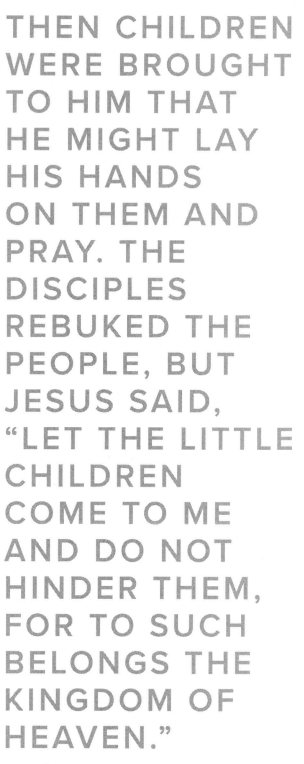

THEN CHILDREN
WERE BROUGHT
TO HIM THAT
HE MIGHT LAY
HIS HANDS
ON THEM AND
PRAY. THE
DISCIPLES
REBUKED THE
PEOPLE, BUT
JESUS SAID,
"LET THE LITTLE
CHILDREN
COME TO ME
AND DO NOT
HINDER THEM,
FOR TO SUCH
BELONGS THE
KINGDOM OF
HEAVEN."

Matthew 19:13-14

While the Old Testament has basically an entire book on parental advice (Proverbs), Jesus didn't speak much about parenting directly. He didn't have a wife and kids; yet as the only begotten Son of our heavenly Father, in whose image we are created, Christ shows us a holy heart full of patience, love, grace, and wisdom.

In the story in Matthew, parents were bringing their babies and children to Jesus. A common practice in that time was to have a holy man or rabbi bless your child. In fact, there are similar traditions today, but the point here isn't about whether or not you should have your child dedicated to the Lord in a church service. The point here is that Jesus made time for and valued these kids. Their hearts and lives were just as important as the grown men and women. He honored the parents and was gentle with the children. He even pointed to them as an example. We can learn three things from His example:

1. Kids are an invaluable blessing.

Whether you have your own or not, when are you prone to see kids as more of a burden than a blessing?

_____

_____

_____

If/when you have kids, what will you do to love them well?

_____

_____

_____

2. We can learn from children.

Look at the awe and wonder of children. What can you learn from their example?

_____

_____

_____

Next time you have to correct, discipline, or deal with something that you don't want to, stop and think about how it relates to your own relationship with God. But here's the great news: your heavenly Father is never too frustrated, busy, or tired for you. He always makes the right decisions, never loses his temper, and always invites you to spend time with him while he works.

What is something that you constantly say to or do for your kids?

_____

_____

_____

What does that teach you about God's love for you?

_____

_____

_____

_____

3. It's our job to introduce them to Jesus.

How are you intentionally teaching your kids about God?

_____

_____

_____

Is there anything you are doing that could keep your child (or other people around you) from seeing the truth about why knowing Jesus really matters?

_____

_____

_____

Like is often the case, Jesus' words likely had literal meaning, "Let the kids come to me, the kingdom of God is for them too," and a symbolic meaning, "A relationship with God requires childlike faith." This doesn't mean naïve or immature and unquestioning; it means that we must be completely dependent upon our Father as children do for all of their needs and find joy in the good gifts He provides. Little kids just want to be in the presence of their parents. They want to see and learn and know that they are noticed and loved.

But it's easy to get impatient with kids or exhausted by their constant need for attention or supervision. So often we just want them to do what they're told. Why won't they listen? Why won't they do what they're told? Why don't they learn from their mistakes? Why do they keep doing that over and over? Don't they know that's bad for them or that they'll get hurt?

You can probably identify with this story, whether or not you have kids of your own. Look at the disciples. They're *rebuking* parents for bothering Jesus with their kids. They probably thought they were doing the important ministry of preaching and healing a favor. The disciples probably weren't being ugly, but *rebuked* is a strong word to indicate that there was zero patience for wasting time dealing with kids.

The same can be true in our culture, where it's sometimes seen as a "value" to be too busy with seemingly important things to recognize the gift of children.

> *As I hung up the phone it occurred to me, my boy was just like me.*
> *Yeah, my boy was just like.*

The ultimate purpose of parenthood is to introduce children to Jesus so that they can grow up to love Him with all of their hearts, minds, souls, and all of their strength. Don't let other priorities get in the way.

You or may or may not be a dad at this point. There are few topics as touchy as parenting. How will you educate, how many extracurricular activities can kids be involved in, how will you discipline, how much sleep should they get, how much screen time is okay, how much sugar is okay, and the list goes on and on. Everyone wants to do the best job possible.

But take a deep breath. Relax. Believe it or not, there's no one-size-fits-all guide to perfect parenting. There's no such thing as the right way for all Christian parents to educate or discipline their kids, for example. But you'll have personal convictions and discernment for what works in your home for each kid. Ultimately, you have to choose what fits into your purpose as a couple and as a family.

God has a plan and knows what he is doing. Whether through adoption, birth, or helping others in the church or community, you have the awesome privilege of loving on kids and helping them know Jesus.

Look back at what you identified as your personal calling and purpose as a couple or family. Write it down here.

_____

_____

What effect does your God-given purpose have on parenting decisions, including if, when, and how many kids you want to have?

_____

_____

Now let's do some general questions on hot topics to help you discuss some of the important with your wife.

1. How many kids would you like to have? _____

2. How would you describe your childhood?

_____

_____

3. What good things from your childhood do you want to pass on in your own family? What examples do you intend to follow?

_____

_____

_____

4. What do you want to avoid and not do as a parent that was a part of your own childhood?

_____

_____

_____

5. What forms of discipline do you think are effective? What is the purpose of discipline?

_____

_____

_____

6. Do you have an opinion on what type of education you prefer (public, private, home, other form of school)?

_____

_____

_____

7. How important is it to be active in a local church? What does it mean in your mind to be active in church?

_____

_____

_____

8. What excites you about kids?

_____

_____

9. What scares you about kids?

_____

_____

10. What specific things do you need prayer for as a husband and father?

_____

_____

_____

For centuries, many Jewish families have affixed a little box or cylinder called a mezuzah to the doorways of their homes. A mezuzah contains a tiny scroll with the words of Deuteronomy 6:4-9 and 11:13-21, the passage of Scripture often referred to as the *Shema*, which is the first word in the original Hebrew language, meaning hear or listen.

This is a beautiful picture of family, parenting, and passing along your faith from one generation to the next. You'll see the mention of doorposts that these traditional Jewish families have taken literally. Read the first half of this Scripture and let it sink deep into your heart. You should also notice the familiar command that Jesus said is most important in life. This has been God's purpose for his people all along.

Listen, Israel: The Lord our God, the Lord is one. Love the Lord your God with all your heart, with all your soul, and with all your strength. These words that I am giving you today are to be in your heart. Repeat them to your children. Talk about them when you sit in your house and when you walk along the road, when you lie down and when you get up. Bind them as a sign on your hand and let them be a symbol on your forehead. Write them on the doorposts of your house and on your city gates.

Deuteronomy 6:4-9 (CSB)

You know the drill by now. Turn off or put down your phones. Give each other all of your attention. This week has another video that clocks in around 45 minutes with Willie Robertson and his wife, Korie, from *Duck Dynasty.* Their hearts for kids are bigger than his world famous beard!

- Sit together and ask each other to name a favorite memory from your own childhood and what made it special.

- Ask one another the ten questions from the list of that can become potential areas of conflict if you don't have clear communication.

- Read the words of Jesus, the Shema, and the proverb, sharing how each of those verses helped you think about children and parenting.

- Ask each other about any of the other things you read and wrote about in the *On Your Own* section on the previous pages. Remember, this is a conversation with your wife. Enjoy it!

- Go to *Love That Lasts* in your library at *bethkeworkshops.com* and watch this week's video: Parenting with Korie and Willie Robertson. Then, ask each other what was most interesting, most challenging, and a big takeaway from the video. Use the video sidebar to take notes and to help your conversation.

- Now is a great time to reconnect with the mentor couple you may have identified in the first session. Invite them over or meet up to ask about parenting and anything that you've read, studied, and discussed since you last got together.

Parenting with

Willie & Korie Robertson

This section is a place to take notes if you also purchased the 12 corresponding video sessions from our 12 mentors. What did they say that resonated with you? What was your favorite part? What was most challenging?

Train up a child in the
way he should go:
even when he is old he
will not depart from it.
Proverbs 22:6

If you don't have this video
you can purchase it at

lovethatlasts.co/videoseries

Money

After we were married, we hadn't totally merged our bank accounts yet, and our finances and our values and how we were going to do it were still in flux. Alyssa was working as a high school counselor at a private Christian school. She loved it, but wasn't making much money.

A month later, we were at a drive-thru and when I pulled up to pay, she put her arm over my arm, as if to stop me from getting my wallet. And with a smirk she says, "Don't worry. Mama's got this." I always wanted to marry a sugar mama so it was a dream come true.

Then a few days later we were at another store and at the register I looked at her and asked, "Mama's got this?"

She answered, "No, mama doesn't got this. If mama gets this, then she'll overdraft."

We just started laughing. But what was fun about those first few months of marriage for us was that we were able to start fresh and set values, goals, and benchmarks for how we wanted to steward money together.

The bedrock of a healthy marriage in regards to finance is understanding what money is for. The way Alyssa and I look at it, money is good but it's not God. It's a tool to be used, not something that should use us. Meaning, we want to use money to give generously, create stability, attain certain dreams and goals. Money provides housing, and electricity, and other things.

The minute we make money our end goal, or the thing we are pursuing at all costs, is the minute something becomes off. It's a tool, and like any tool, it can be used poorly or it can be used well.

This was really helpful for us to understand, because early on in marriage we felt pressure to make our financial systems look very traditional—a strict budget, a balance sheet, checkbook, and all of that.

But we realized that didn't really work well for us. As authors and YouTubers, the money is very inconsistent and it comes over long periods of time in random places and dates. It became difficult for us to set certain budgets and goals in the micro. For us, going big picture though was deeply helpful. We started setting really big picture rules in this order:

1. Set aside money for giving first.
2. Pay bills.
3. Save.
4. Keep the rest in a cash flow account that was for our daily expenses.

Simple, but really effective for us. Another thing we do with part of the money we'd set aside to give, is to give to marriages and families. So in our community we'd hear of someone who needed a crib, or had some friends we wanted to send on a date night, then we'd take from that account.

There's something that happens when we give. It's contagious and creates so much joy in us—more than if we spent it on ourselves. But then also a lot of times it'd spark a chain reaction in the other people to do the same. Imagine how much joy and love we are kept from by not being generous.

Ask yourself and your spouse, what money is to you. And then make a plan, maybe small picture or big picture, in regards to how you will deal with it. And live within your means. Doing that for us has a profound effect on our marriage, because we are rarely stressing since we have put our expenses per month lower than our income. Making those numbers too close per month is a recipe for stress, not joy. Let's choose the latter.

Write your favorite quote, song lyric, or Bible verse related to money or contentment. If you're extra artistic, get creative with your handwriting or draw something to represent success.

GUIDEBOOK

Money

"DON'T STORE UP
FOR YOURSELVES
TREASURES ON
EARTH BUT STORE ...
UP FOR YOURSELVES
TREASURES IN
HEAVEN ...
FOR WHERE YOUR
TREASURE IS, THERE
YOUR HEART WILL
BE ALSO ...
NO ONE CAN SERVE
TWO MASTERS,
SINCE EITHER HE WILL
HATE ONE AND LOVE
THE OTHER, OR HE
WILL BE DEVOTED TO
ONE AND DESPISE
THE OTHER. YOU
CANNOT SERVE BOTH
GOD AND MONEY."

Matthew 6:19-21, 24 (CSB)

Notice that Jesus didn't say that you can't have both God and money. He doesn't even say that you can't *enjoy* both God and money. Jesus said that you can't serve both God and money. They can't both be your master, which is what the term *Lord* means. You have to choose one.

The master you work for and the treasure you are seeking are either temporal or eternal in nature. One can be taken and lost, but the other lasts forever. Jesus is asking you to choose which is better: heaven or earth, God or money. When we step back to see the full picture, it's easy to see which one is the better choice. But it's hard when we don't have the big picture in view. Or when we have bills due.

So ask yourself, where is your ultimate allegiance? What are you working for? And then keep your priorities in mind when it comes to creating, and sticking to, your budget together.

When you have a tough decision and it comes down to money or a sense of conviction, what do you do?

Pray about it:	first	during	after	never
Think about money:	first	during	after	never

How important is money to you?

1	·	2	·	3	·	4	·	5	·	6	·	7	·	8	·	9	·	10

Not at all   *It consumes me*

How important is God's purpose for you?

1 · 2 · 3 · 4 · 5 · 6 · 7 · 8 · 9 · 10

Not at all   *It consumes me*

What do the answers above reveal about your treasure and master?

_____

_____

If someone looked at your bank statements what would they most likely think (i.e. you eat out frequently, go shopping, give generously, etc)?

_____

_____

Based on the purpose you identified for your life in session 8 (pg 175), does the way you handle money reflect intentionality in pursuing your purpose?

_____

_____

What can you do to take steps toward handling your money more intentionally to pursue your purpose?

_____

_____

Storing up treasures in heaven doesn't simply mean that you refuse to be openly greedy or to engage in sketchy business practices; it means that your God-given purpose is the guiding principle for your life and decisions—including how you make, save, give, and spend money.

ON YOUR OWN

One thing you'll notice as you compare notes with your wife and if you watch the video is that there are often differences between marriages and also within marriages on attitudes toward money.

Most likely, there is a *spender* and a *saver* in your marriage; but it's also possible to have two *spenders* or two *savers* in a relationship.

I am a:	spender	saver
My wife is a:	spender	saver

What problems can arise if both people are *spenders?*

_____

_____

What problems can arise if both people are *savers?*

_____

_____

What problems can arise is one person is a *spender* and one is a *saver?*

_____

_____

In your own marriage, where do problems or conflicts about money arise?

_____

_____

How do you try to balance one another when it comes to money?

_____

_____

What do you enjoy spending money on?

_____

_____

What do you hate spending money on?

_____

_____

When do you get stressed about money?

_____

_____

How are you generous with your money?

_____

_____

It's helpful to consider how you grew up when trying to understand the way that you and your wife view money.

How would you describe your financial situation growing up?

1 · 2 · 3 · 4 · 5 · 6 · 7 · 8 · 9 · 10

Poor   *Rich*

Who worked:	dad	mom	kids
	step-dad	step-mom	other:

How often was money discussed in your home?

1 · 2 · 3 · 4 · 5 · 6 · 7 · 8 · 9 · 10

Never   *Nonstop*

How would you describe the general attitude toward money in your home growing up? What sort of money-related things were discussed?

_____

_____

Describe your expectation of what life would look like when it came to a home, car, income, vacation, shopping, social life, etc?

_____

_____

_____

Are there any areas in your life where you intend to use your money differently than the way it was used in the home you grew up in? If so, what are they and why do you want to treat those things differently?

_____

_____

_____

_____

What is your most important financial priority?

_____

_____

Now you may or may not have a strict budget, depending on your sources of income and various obligations, but it's important to get at least a general picture of your money—where it comes from and where it goes.

The questions above will help you understand yourself and each other better when it comes to how you view money. Your conversation about those things will increase healthy communication and enable you to better navigate potential conflict—hopefully even avoid some conflict altogether!

This final activity will give you something to work with when you get together with your wife. This will be a very practical tool. Feel free to be as detailed as you want or need to be based on your personality and your financial realities. Under each category, you may want to get detail—breaking down housing, for example, into rent or mortgage, utilities, maintenance, etc. Or you may just want round numbers. Either way, make sure the numbers are realistic, even if not perfect. The key is to get at least a framework sketched out so that you and your wife can be on the same page.

HUSBAND'S INCOME	WIFE'S INCOME
TITHE / GIVING	SAVINGS
HOUSING	SPENDING
TRANSPORTATION	OTHER

You know the drill by now. Turn off or put down your phones. Give each other all of your attention. This week ...

- Sit together and talk about some of the jobs you've worked. What did you want to be when you grew up? What was your first job? Worst job? Best job? Strangest or funniest thing to happen at work? Have you ever had any jobs you stayed in just because of the money? Or jobs you loved, but they made money really tight?

- Read the words of Jesus, the Shema, and the proverb, sharing how each of those verses helped you think about money.

- Ask each other about questions and exercises you did in the *On Your Own* section on the previous pages. Remember, this is a conversation with your wife. Get to know her. Listen. Enjoy it!

- Compare your budgets. Did you both do simple or detailed budgets? Talk through the basic realities, obligations, and priorities of how you handle money. Fill in the *Our Money Snapshot* to get a general picture of your finances. Be sure the numbers add up to a realistic lifestyle.

- Go to *Love That Lasts* in your library at *bethkeworkshops.com* and watch this week's video: Money with Matt and Jayne Shatto. They've made money and stewarded it very well, and specifically offer creative ways to walk through the topic of money. After the video, ask each other what was most interesting, most challenging, and a big takeaway from the video. Use the video sidebar to take notes and to help your conversation.

The goal here is not to provide a strategy for handling your money, other than to be wise, communicate with one another, and be intentional to pursue your purpose in loving God and others. You may have separate bank accounts; you may share. You may put cash in envelopes; you may use apps to track your spending. There are all kinds of ways to honor God and handle your money with integrity.

So instead of a strategy, the point here is to get a snapshot.

HUSBAND'S INCOME	WIFE'S INCOME
TITHE / GIVING	SAVINGS
HOUSING	SPENDING
TRANSPORTATION	OTHER

Finances with

Matt & Jayne Shatto

This section is a place to take notes if you also purchased the
12 corresponding video sessions from our 12 mentors. What did
they say that resonated with you? What was your favorite part?
What was most challenging?

A greedy person stirs
up conflict,
but whoever trusts in
the Lord will prosper.
Proverbs 28:25 (CSB)

If you don't have this video
you can purchase it at

lovethatlasts.co/videoseries

Boundaries

10

Our little girl, Kinsley, is one of the most fearless three-year-olds you will ever meet. She wants to completely charge life with everything she has. This means her transportation of choice is usually running. I sometimes if she even knows that walking is an actual option, or if she thinks running is just how legs are meant to work.

Her current favorite thing is going outside after dinner and skateboarding or scootering. I ordered some kneepads and elbow pads, which haven't showed up yet, but that hasn't deterred her. Last night she took two decent falls. At first I was nervous I'd hear a cry begin just moments after the fall (parents almost have a sixth sense for this stuff). Instead, both times she got up and said, "Wow! Fast, Daddy!" She was so stoked with herself and how fast she had gone, she had pretty much forgotten the fall already.

But one of the big things we are trying to teach her right now, especially because she's so fearless, is to have healthy boundaries. What is appropriate and what isn't. With skateboarding, we are teaching her to look both ways before she enters the street. Also she can't ride without a helmet, and she can't be out there without a parent.

These boundaries that are actually not just for her safety, but for her freedom. True freedom always involves healthy boundaries. It's what creates it. False freedom is having none. Take, for example, skydiving. You can enjoy the full freedom of falling from the sky, because of the restraint of the parachute. Try to make yourself more "free" without that, and it's not true freedom because you'll die.

In every healthy relationship, each person and couple needs to set up good boundaries in order for the relationship to thrive. There are obvious boundaries like not dating other people and not having an affair, but those things don't just happen overnight. They take time and a lot of forethought. So what boundaries can you put in place to not only protect you as a couple, but to give life to your relationship?

Some general rules are helpful but some can be very specific to you two and how you operate and what's best to make you two thrive as a couple. Here are a few practical things that Alyssa and I have implemented in our marriage to protect our unity, purity, and joy:

1. Refuse to speak poorly about each other in public or private. This one is big for me. We've often been in a room where a husband degrades his wife, who's in the room, in front of others. It's mortifying for everyone there. Or other times a wife can sometimes belittle her husband when she's with her girlfriends. Words set standards and build foundations. And you can create death or you can create life. One of the markers of a strong marriage is strong and encouraging words about each other, to each other, and in front of others.

2. Set up intentional time. This is different depending on the day but we try to have some form of intentional communication every single day. If we don't do that, we notice each other start to drift and grow distant. Even if it's five minutes before the kids wake up, we say, "Hey, how are you really doing this morning?"

3. No secrets. Ever. No marriage has even been encouraged and served by one spouse holding secrets from the other (except for that time I surprised Alyssa with a trip to NYC to see Hamilton, but surprises for a spouse are different than keeping secrets from her). We live in a way where we aren't going to hide texts from our spouse, lie about something we did that day, and so on. Secrets destroy a marriage. And committing to no secrets is one of the best ways to safeguard against that, and also build incredible trust and intimacy.

4. **Know what gives life to you and your spouse, and what drains it.** This one Alyssa and I are still learning, and getting better at each year. And this will morph with us as seasons change. This has to do more with your time and energy level. Every couple is different. Some of us are extroverts, and others introverts. We all need different things and go at different paces. A lot of times one person gets burned out because the other isn't respecting boundaries. Talk about this with your spouse, and find a good way to know when to say yes to things, when to say no, or when to take a rain check. Should you have that family over for dinner? When? How long should your house guests stay with you? Do you need to get a house cleaner so you don't have to be so exhausted after? Should you commit to another activity, a small group, take on another part time job, another payment plan? How can you set yourselves up for rest, joy, and success? If you're drowning in some way, feeling exhausted, disconnected, then what needs to change?

GUIDEBOOK

Boundaries

10

THEY ASKED HIM, "LORD, ARE YOU RESTORING THE KINGDOM TO ISRAEL AT THIS TIME?"

HE SAID TO THEM, "IT IS NOT FOR YOU TO KNOW TIMES OR PERIODS THAT THE FATHER HAS SET BY HIS OWN AUTHORITY. BUT YOU WILL RECEIVE POWER WHEN THE HOLY SPIRIT HAS COME ON YOU, AND YOU WILL BE MY WITNESSES IN JERUSALEM, IN ALL JUDEA AND SAMARIA, AND TO THE END OF THE EARTH."

Acts 1:6-8 (CSB)

The disciples were talking to Jesus forty days after He had raised from the dead. Clearly God was doing something unprecedented. All of the promises they had read in Scripture were coming true. While we know that they were still missing the point of what was happening, their question was more than fair. They're trying to understand. They're excited. They're confused. And any faithful Jew was looking forward to God's kingdom, which Jesus spoke a lot about by the way. (The disciples are so ordinary! It should be really encouraging if you ever wonder if you're good enough or capable of God working in and through your life for His awesome purpose!)

Jesus says that the disciples have a great purpose: They will be His witnesses. They will receive the Holy Spirit. But they don't need to know or worry about all the details—not even the end goal. Jesus didn't say their question was a bad one; it just wasn't one they needed to worry about.

Here's where we see the importance of boundaries, even in good things, in living out God's purpose for your life. Jesus gave them a direction and set a boundary. Don't get sidetracked over here with God's timing. Stay focused on your next steps of obedience in faith. Trust God to do his thing. You do yours.

Boundaries aren't always about sin. Sometimes they're about focus.

What good things distract your attention from what's most important?

_____

_____

_____

What drains your energy and sidetracks you from the purpose you identified for your life?

_____

_____

_____

_____

_____

Alyssa and I like to say that if your romantic relationship is healthy and flourishing, everything else follows. But if it's unhealthy and hurtful and not giving life, then it doesn't matter if everything else is. In some ways, relationships affect everything else in our lives. They are the epicenter that ripples out to everything else. How we view relationships, how we trust the Lord in them, and how we walk with Him affects how we live our life, how we do our jobs, and how we grow.

It's possible that you need a change of perspective about boundaries. Many of us do. When you first read the word *boundary,* what's your immediate connotation?

positive	negative	neutral

Boundaries are ultimately about protecting what you value. That sounds obvious, but as humans we naturally resist the idea of boundaries. Think back at the story of Adam and Eve again. Everybody knows this part of the story. Adam and Eve are naked and happy in the garden. Life is perfect. God has blessed them and said that they can enjoy everything he has created. There is literally only one boundary set in the universe. The fruit of one tree is off limits. One. And they take it. Bite it. Share it. Together. They believe the lie that joy and freedom are found in a life without boundaries.

We still believe the lie of the serpent that real freedom means doing whatever we want. We want to do what we think is best, regardless of what God may have said. But God clearly sets boundaries for our own good. You wouldn't tell your own kids that they could do whatever they think would make them happy. You need to trust your heavenly Father that he knows what is best for you. Boundaries and order allow things to flourish. He wants you to experience joy.

What boundaries have you currently set in your own life to avoid personal temptation and sin?

_____

_____

_____

What boundaries have you set in your marriage to protect your love?

_____

_____

_____

Being "one" in marriage doesn't mean you have no life or interests of your own. It's healthy and important to have some time to recharge with things you enjoy. Maybe you like to run or workout. Maybe you enjoy basketball or kayaking. Maybe you just need some time at home to read or to work on furniture. It's not selfish to spend a reasonable amount of time doing those things—it's actually good for your marriage.

This is actually a healthy boundary—guarding some time as an outlet and refueling of personal energy. But that same boundary works both ways. Make sure you protect a reasonable amount of time for "your" thing, but don't cross that boundary either, taking too much "me" time.

The key is that the amount of time you spend on "your thing" isn't disproportionate to the amount of time you spend together and that you both agree on what that looks like in your own marriage.

If you're always out with your friends or by yourself, your spouse begins to feel neglected and eventually resentful. Make sure the other person is the priority for your time and energy, but don't stop doing (or discovering) things that you enjoy. Encourage your spouse to take time to do the same.

What do you like to do?

_____

_____

_____

How much time do you spend doing that thing/those things?

_____

_____

_____

What does your wife enjoy?

_____

_____

_____

How much time does she spend?

_____

_____

_____

How much time is a reasonable amount for you both to spend on personal interests?

_____

_____

_____

The important thing with boundaries is that they both protect against things that would be bad for you and your marriage, and ensure areas of freedom in things that are good and life-giving. A good gardener—even an all-natural, organic farmer—doesn't allow anything and everything to grow together. A gardener sets boundaries, cultivating growth and health, preventing other things from choking out the good stuff. In other words, boundaries are a good thing. Work with your wife to set healthy boundaries that encourage you to flourish as individuals, as a couple, and as a family.

JOIN
TOGETHER

Yep. Time to turn off or put down your phones. Give each other all of your attention.

- Sit together and pray for clarity and transparency for ways to serve one another by protecting each other's hearts and time. Thank God for the gift of someone who loves you so well.
- Read the words of Jesus and the proverb, sharing how each of those verses helped you think about money.
- Ask each other about questions and exercises you did in the *On Your Own* section on the previous pages. Remember, this is a conversation with your wife. Get to know her. Be honest. Listen carefully. Enjoy it!
- Share with one another what you thought about the suggestions for setting healthy boundaries. What would these look like in your own marriage?

  - ➡ Keep communicating.
  - ➡ Refuse to speak poorly about each other.
  - ➡ No secrets. Ever.
  - ➡ Set up intentional time.
  - ➡ Know what gives life to you and your spouse, and what drains it.
  - ➡ Be wise. Know your triggers.

- What new boundaries need to be set to intentionally focus your lives on God's purpose for you?
- Go to *Love That Lasts* in your library at *bethkeworkshops.com* and watch this week's video: Boundaries with Dave and Ashley Willis. Then ask each other what was most interesting, most challenging, and a big takeaway from the video. Use the video sidebar to take notes and to help your conversation.

Boundaries with

Dave & Ashley Willis

This section is a place to take notes if you also purchased the
12 corresponding video sessions from our 12 mentors. What did
they say that resonated with you? What was your favorite part?
What was most challenging?

By wisdom a house is built,
and by understanding it is
established; by knowledge
the rooms are filled with all
precious and pleasant riches.

Proverbs 24:3-4

If you don't have this video
you can purchase it at

lovethatlasts.co/videoseries

Addiction

11

Idols are one of the most destructive things to any marriage. This includes anything we elevate to the place of God, that isn't God. This can be good things—our job, our spouse, our kids. Or bad things— porn, alcohol, narcissism. But the fact remains, if we put anything as the ultimate pursuit of our life, and it's not Jesus, it can't sustain that weight. It won't be able to hold the pressure.

And honestly this isn't a new problem. When you read the first page of scripture, you see this was the same decision Adam and Eve had. They could trust God and lean on Him for goodness, beauty, wisdom, and life. Or they could try to find life and beauty in other things.

They chose the latter, and ever since there has been a fracturing through the cosmos. A curse in our lives, jobs, and relationships—where the curse came from in the first place.

We all have something we are prone to worship more than Jesus— ourselves, a substance, sex, a job, and so on. But in a marriage, these things can wreak havoc.

I know of countless marriages that have ended because a husband worshiped naked bodies on a computer, more than following Jesus and loving his wife.

I know of marriages that have ended because the husband loved their job more Jesus.

I know of marriages that have ended because the husband loved their comfort more than Jesus.

One of the critical things we have to do in our marriages is make them idol-proof. Another way I've heard it put is to go idol hunting. We need to seek out and make note of the very things that most tempt us or distract our relationship with Jesus and our marriages. When your marriage isn't in a good spot, what is usually the common theme?

Or, what's your full moon? I heard a friend say that everyone has a werewolf in them, but everyone has different things that turn them into that werewolf. It's helpful to discuss those things with your spouse so you can take practical steps to help each other. Pray for each other. Put in the hard work of grace and repentance each day that brings healing.

A lot of dealing with idols comes down to a proper understanding of what it means when Jesus says the word *kingdom.* Often when we hear the word *kingdom* or *heaven,* we think of a place really far away that we go to when we die. But according to Jewish thought, the world Jesus lived in, heaven was actually more like God's control room. God's space. A place that is near.

When Jesus steps on the scene, He tells people to turn around, change their mind, and change the direction of their lives because the place where God is fully reigning and ruling is near. It is right in front of them, in Jesus. It's less about a destination and more about bringing our lives under His reign and rule right now. In this moment. In our finances, in our schools, in our relationships, and every facet of our being.

If you had to describe who was in control of your life, who would it be? Jesus? You? An idol? The beautiful invitation we have in Jesus is to come near to Him and bring our lives under His beautiful and glorious reign. And that's the place we experience joy, forgiveness, beauty, and shalom.

You are good enough because God sees you through the eyes of Jesus. He covers you. You are worthy because Jesus died for you: He loved you that much and thought you were worth it. Regardless of what type of home you grew up in, what your story is growing up, you have to face these questions and you can face them head on if you have Jesus. Let His word be the final word. You are loved. You are worth it. You are enough. He is so proud of you. He delights in you. You are His.

GUIDEBOOK

Addiction

BUT SEEK
FIRST THE
KINGDOM
OF GOD
AND HIS
RIGHTEOUS-
NESS, AND
ALL THESE
THINGS
WILL BE
PROVIDED
FOR YOU.

Matthew 6:33 (CSB)

In Jesus' greatest sermon, what we call the Sermon on the Mount, He uncovers a wide spectrum of heart issues. He goes idol hunting, shedding light on some of the dark corners of our hearts and minds. Ultimately, stress, worry, addiction, and sin have their roots in worship.

The things we keep going back to, the things that have power in our lives, things that often feel uncontrollable, are things we worship. They're idols. Something inside of us believes the lie that satisfaction, relief, happiness, purpose, acceptance, etc. will be found in this thing other than our Creator. This is the original lie of the serpent in the Garden of Eden. There's a sinful bent in our hearts that doesn't believe that God is good enough. He's holding back on us. We just can't stand the thought of not biting that forbidden fruit. It looks so good.

In Matthew 5-6, Jesus pounds idol after idol:

☐ Logic and common sense (5:1-12).

☐ Blending in (5:13-16).

☐ Self-righteousness (5:17-20).

☐ Hate and unforgiveness (5:21-26).

☐ Lust (5:27-30).

☐ Selfishness, convenience, personal rights (5:31-48)

☐ Charitable recognition (6:1-4).

☐ Religious recognition (6:5-18).

☐ Money, success, and possessions (6:19-24).

☐ Food, drink, clothing, physical appearance (6:25-34).

Idol after idol after idol, Jesus says that he has something infinitely greater for us. These things that seem so appealing easily seduce our hearts. But Jesus offers us more: He offers true and lasting satisfaction.

Throughout these chapters, Jesus says, "your heavenly Father who sees in secret." God knows. He knows what you think, feel, do, and why you think feel, and do it. He knows your heart.

The fact that Jesus loves me even though he knows my secret idols makes me feel...

positive	negative

On the previous page, put a check next to the idols you tend to worship.

The verse quoted at the beginning of this section is Jesus' response to our desire for food, drink, and clothing. Jesus says that to put any of these things at the center of our hearts and minds, obsessing over them, worrying about them, seeking them, is a godless thing to do. He promises over and over that God is a perfectly good and generous Father who knows what we need. (Part of knowing our secrets is not only knowing our motives but also our needs.) Jesus promises that if we'll focus our hearts on the goodness of God, seeking his righteousness, first and foremost in our lives, then our heavenly Father will take care of all the things we need and that will give us joy.

He doesn't say food, drink, clothing, wealth, sex, charity, etc. are bad. He says that when our focus is on finding meaning and security in those things instead of in him, everything gets bent out of whack. When we can't stop obsessing over them, they'll ruin us. When they become our masters, we'll become enslaved to them. This isn't to be taken lightly or dismissed as a nobody-is-perfect kind of thing. Sin and idolatry are a big, big deal. Look at what Jesus said in the same chapter:

> *If your right eye causes you to sin, gouge it out and throw it away. For it is better that you lose one of the parts of your body than for your whole body to be thrown into hell. And if your right hand causes you to sin, cut it off and throw it away. For it is better that you lose one of the parts of your body than for your whole body to go into hell.*
> *Matthew 5:29-30 (CSB)*

That's intense, but sin is no joke. It's a lie to believe that "as long as I'm not hurting anybody else, then it's not a big deal," or "as long as I only look or think but don't act, it's OK." No. Jesus said to do whatever you have to do to break free from sinful strongholds in your life.

Write a quote, song lyric, or Bible verse related to addiction. If you're extra artistic, get creative with your handwriting or draw something to represent addiction or idolatry.

There are seasons where things are going well—you're passionate about God and aware of His activity; relationships are strong; work is satisfying; and free time is enjoyable. When the blessings of God are evident, revel in the freedom and joy of Christ. Each minute is dripping with grace. Soak it up so that you are saturated with peace and spreading His love everywhere you go.

But other days, months, or even years, feel like those same minutes are a suffocating weight under which you are desperately trying to catch a breath that will fill your lungs long enough to sustain you until rescue arrives. It may be easy to believe in your mind that God is good and sovereign, but that doesn't mean you won't find yourself in painful and unfair situations, exhausted, confused, hurting, and at the end of your rope. So what then?

A good way to identify idols and addictions is to look at your patterns of thought or behavior that pop up when you're stressed or drained. Essentially these habitual behaviors have become "functional saviors" that you have an idolatrous love for. You want these idols to validate you, help you, save you. In other words, you look to them for *salvation.*

What do you turn to or "need" when you're under stress?

_____

_____

_____

Underline things that have been past struggles.

Circle current temptations.

Food	Games
Drink	Technology
Drugs	Shopping
Sex	Exercise
Pornography	Work
People	Validation
Social Media	Other:
TV / Movies	

When your marriage isn't in a good spot, what is usually the common theme?

_____

_____

What triggers typically set off addictive patterns or temptations?

_____

_____

_____

What areas of your life do you still need to bring under God's reign and rule?

_____

_____

_____

What boundaries do you need to set—and ask for your wife's help in protecting—to stay focused on God's goodness, His righteousness, His kingdom instead of idolatrous desires and functional saviors?

_____

_____

_____

JOIN
TOGETHER

Turn off or put down your phones. (If you haven't noticed, there are surprisingly powerful and addictive behaviors that develop from our phones. How often do you look at them? How hard has it been each week to set them down without looking at them? Do you notice a difference in yourself when you spend more or less time on your phone? Just something to consider.)

Give each other all of your attention. This week is a heavy one, but it's so important.

Some form of addictive behavior has wrecked countless lives and marriages. It's not always something like substance abuse; sometimes it's something like working or neglecting your family because you're always on your phone. But the mentor couple in this week's video will share the difficult road of struggling, confessing, and recovering from an addiction to pornography while in full time ministry. Nobody is bullet proof. Everyone has a target on his back from the enemy, and there's nothing more dangerous than pretending like it isn't there.

- Sit together on the couch or at the table. If you have Jenga, play it for a few minutes for at least one round. If you can't play it, picture the game in your mind and ask each other to explain how the game is played. This is a simple illustration that may be a little cheesy but a fun way to start a tougher topic.

    → The point of the illustration is that each of you has something that may be fine in moderation but could eventually become a problem—even one that could destroy your life and your marriage.

    → Sometimes one slip is all it take to cause a major problem.

- → The game has a mixture of fear and adrenaline as you feel compelled to keep doing something. It feels like you're getting away with something every time you don't get busted. This is a great picture of addiction and sinful patterns.
- → No matter how good you think you are at handling it—whatever it may be—eventually things will come crashing down. It may be an emotional crash. It could be spiritual. Physical. Relational. Financial. Professional. Legal. But there will always be a crash if we keep playing with destructive patterns.
- → We need to encourage one another to stop when we see a pattern that is destructive. Life isn't a game. Cleaning up isn't easy. But if messes have been made in the past, commit to help one another build and guard a new foundation for starting fresh. (This takes trust, communication, and boundaries to a new level of intimacy.)

- Pray together, thanking God for his unconditional love and grace. Ask for Him to fill your hearts with love for Him and for each other in this time of serving one another through compassion and honesty.
- Read the words of Jesus and the proverb, sharing how each of those verses helped you think about addictions.
- Ask each other about questions and exercises you did in the *On Your Own* section on the previous pages. Remember, this is a conversation with your wife. Get to know her. When she speaks, don't try to "fix." Listen. When you're sharing, be honest and vulnerable. She loves you. You can trust her.
- This is important. Specifically, ask about temptations, patterns, triggers, and common themes when things are bad.

- Help each other identify healthy boundaries to guard one another's hearts and minds so that you can seek the goodness and freedom of life under the authority of a loving Father and King.

- Go to *Love That Lasts* in your library at *bethkeworkshops.com* and watch this week's video: Addiction with Bernie and Christina Anderson. Then ask each other what was most interesting, most challenging, and a big takeaway from the video. Use the video sidebar to take notes and to help your conversation.

- Be sure to make note of the resources linked under the video for more insights on specific issues. These are invaluable resources for you and for people you know.

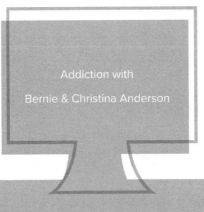

Addiction with

Bernie & Christina Anderson

This section is a place to take notes if you also purchased the 12 corresponding video sessions from our 12 mentors. What did they say that resonated with you? What was your favorite part? What was most challenging?

_____

_____

_____

_____

_____

_____

_____

_____

_____

_____

_____

_____

Can a man embrace fire and his clothes not be burned?
Can a man walk on burning coals without scorching his feet?
Proverbs 6:27-28 (CSB)

If you don't have this video
you can purchase it at

lovethatlasts.co/videoseries

Rhythms

12

In my opinion one of the most overlooked things needed for a healthy marriage (and family) is the establishing of rhythms. In many ways, the industrial revolution has created a overworked and under-rested society, one that no longer has any sense of rhythm. Stores are open 24 hours a day. People check email while they are in bed at night at 11pm. Family dinners are a thing of the past. Humanity is an assembly line.

But for the most of human history, people lived with a sense of rhythm. Day and night. Day and night. Weeks. Then months. Then years. Sabbaths. Gathering around the table nightly to share stories, food, and love. In many cultures before us, there was a respect for the fact that the universe operated on a rhythm whether we liked it or not. And stepping into that rhythm, just like a song, means submitting to the music and stepping in line with *how it's supposed to be*.

For our family, the center of rhythms is rest. If you don't know how to have a rhythm of rest, then you probably won't have a rhythm of intimacy, date nights, dinners, and other rhythmic goals you'd like to have. It starts with rest because we were created for it. Sabbath is in our bones.

And when I say rest, I don't mean sitting back on the couch, drinking a beer, and watching a football game all day. And I certainly don't mean running errands all day because it's your "off day," and then going home and crashing as if you are more tired than a normal work day.

At the heart of rest is enjoyment. Enjoyment of each other, God, life, outdoors, food, neighbors, and our kids. We were created to see life through the rhythm of rest.

Rest is on the first page of the scriptures. God creates worlds and stars and skies and the sun and the moon and humans. Then he rests, which in the Jewish tradition was better defined as an invitation. An invitation to celebrate, to usher in shalom.

Notice what it must have been like for Adam and Eve. God did all the work, then created them last, then it was the day of rest. So from Adam and Eve's perspective, the first thing they knew was rest. The minute they opened their eyes, it was all done. Nothing more to be created or worked toward. Only an invitation to celebration and play. Their first breath was an invite to the divine's playground of shalom.

Rest is in our very bones. We are to enter into rest, and then be able to work well. If you try to work to get to the rest, you've got it backwards.

Our marriages should reflect this as well. Establishing rhythms in the home and in the covenant is an anchor to the marriage. Markers in time to constantly bring the covenant and love and two parties involved back to a center, a grounding. This could sometimes mean a weekly date night. This could mean family dinners at the table with no phones or devices every night. Or our personal favorite is a weekly Sabbath where we shut off our phones, play, eat well, and celebrate each other. But the important thing is hashing it out with your spouse and asking what serves your marriage best? What serves your kids best? What gives you life? The fun part about rhythms is that they get to be unique to you and your marriage. It's not always a question about what is the rule. It's about what serves the relationship.

For example, Alyssa and I try to practice a weekly Sabbath as a family. We have some friends who really encouraged us to take a Sabbath and learn what it means to truly celebrate and play and set apart a day for ceasing each week. But they also encouraged us to think of some specific things that were particular to our family that would represent Sabbath. So in our family we have a couple Bethke traditions that we do every week. One of the biggest is I turn my phone off for that day. Not everyone we know who does a sabbath does this. But for us, it's mandatory. My job is my phone. Youtube. Emails. Twitter. Facebook. I crave the rhythm of turning it off each week. Resetting. Stopping. Realizing my identity isn't in this little glowing screen in my pocket, or my life isn't defined or wrapped up in every thing happening through that glass window.

Another is right before dinner I take an opportunity to look each of our kids in the eye and speak a blessing over them as well as specifically admonish them with how thankful I am for them, how much I love them, and what beautiful things I saw in them that week.

These rhythms become anchors to our family. A way to mark the days and months and years. And also, the universe is playing music. It goes better for us if we recognize that and step into the symphony, rather than pretend it doesn't exist.

Rhythms

12

BUT THE NEWS ABOUT [JESUS] SPREAD EVEN MORE, AND LARGE CROWDS WOULD COME TOGETHER TO HEAR HIM AND TO BE HEALED OF THEIR SICKNESSES. YET HE OFTEN WITHDREW TO DESERTED PLACES AND PRAYED.

Luke 5:15-16 (CSB)

Not only was Jesus a busy and important man, He was God. Yet, Jesus often withdrew to deserted places and prayed. The whole idea that we're too busy to pray or to spend time quietly resting in the presence of God is absurd. No matter what is on your checklist for the day, week, month, or year, it isn't miraculously healing and teaching to mobs of people who follow you around.

The fact that Jesus was God doesn't make the constant demand on His time and energy any less human. He grew tired. But notice the fact that Jesus was God didn't mean He felt exempt from the need to have this pattern of public and private time. Jesus had a steady rhythm in his life. Steady doesn't necessarily mean structured to the point of never changing His daily routine. But His rhythm was one of loving God and loving the people around Him. Love God. Love people. Love God by loving people. Love people by loving God.

Sometimes the most loving thing we can do for people is to spend time alone with God for a bit before returning to them. Jesus didn't stay in the deserted places, but He often withdrew from the public into privacy.

To stress the importance of having healthy spiritual rhythms, consider the first part of the verses above. Jesus was healing people and teaching huge crowds the truth about God. It would've been the world's greatest conference and Bible study! What could be more important than the Son of God healing people and preaching the truth of the kingdom? Sometimes, according to Jesus, being alone in personal prayer was more important than being with the crowds.

The only Son of God. In His short life on earth and a mere three-year ministry. With the power to heal, cast out demons, and even raise the dead. Sometimes the best use of Jesus' time was to be alone. Praying. This was a rhythm in his life and ministry.

Write your favorite quote, song lyric, or Bible verse related to rhythm, longevity, or beauty. If you're extra artistic, get creative with your handwriting or draw something to represent rest, joy, or life.

Once again we can look all the way back to the first pages of Scripture to see this beautiful truth of the God-given gift of rhythms. In fact we look back to the very first hours, so to speak.

In creation we see God establish and bless two rhythms. First we read over and over in Genesis 1, *There was an evening, and there was a morning: one day.* Two. Three. Four. Five. Six. Day after day there is this rhythm and order to all of creation. Dark. Light. Quiet. Activity. Good. Good. Good. Good. Good. Good.

And then this song builds to its crescendo.

> So the heavens and the earth and everything in them were completed. On the seventh day God had completed his work that he had done, and he rested on the seventh day from all his work that he had done. God blessed the seventh day and declared it holy, for on it he rested from all his work of creation.
> Genesis 2:1-3 (CSB)

The most significant part of a rhythm, what defines it, what makes it beautiful, setting it apart from all other noise is the intentional rest. Without the rest, it's just sound. It's noise. It's chaos. But rest breaks up the frenzy of activity into something meaningful. Suddenly it makes sense. It takes a shape and moves our hearts. Noise becomes music.

God created you to flourish as a person created in His image. It's vital to break up the noise in your life with intentional rest. Establish rhythms—personally and in your marriage. If you have kids, establish family rhythms too.

Describe your ideal day (ideal but real-life scenario).

_____

_____

_____

Now describe your typical day.

_____

_____

_____

What natural patterns do you have in your day?

_____

_____

_____

What moments of rest and focus can you add to your routine to bring order and meaning to your day?

_____

_____

_____

Do you regularly practice the following things? If so, when?

pray ◇◇◇◇◇◇◇◇◇◇◇◇◇◇◇◇◇◇◇◇◇◇◇◇ when _____

read the Bible ◇◇◇◇◇◇◇◇◇◇◇◇◇◇◇◇ when _____

worship in a church ◇◇◇◇◇◇◇◇◇◇◇◇ when _____

share life in a small group ◇◇◇◇◇◇◇ when _____

practice generosity ◇◇◇◇◇◇◇◇◇◇◇◇◇ when _____

eat together ◇◇◇◇◇◇◇◇◇◇◇◇◇◇◇◇◇◇ when _____

mentor / disciple ◇◇◇◇◇◇◇◇◇◇◇◇◇◇ when _____

other: _____ when _____

other: _____ when _____

other: _____ when _____

The seventh day of the week, the holy day God blessed is called the *Sabbath.* In the original Hebrew language, the word means to cease. The point here is not about a legalistic practice of not doing certain things on a certain day. The heart of Sabbath is rest and worship. It's focusing our hearts on God. He is the one who created everything. We can trust him enough to be rest in his goodness. Sabbath isn't lazy or legalistic; it's an organic liturgy. It's a natural ordering of our worship through rhythms in life.

Over the past 12 weeks, you've been developing rhythms. You've read on your own, thought through things on your own, and spent time with each other (hopefully without phones or distractions). You've had fun and probably had some difficult spots too. That's good. Most important, we hope that these rhythms have led you to meaningful conversations and deeper intimacy, loving God and loving one another with all of your hearts, minds, souls, and strength.

- Sit together and talk about your favorite rhythms as a couple or family. Share why you enjoy those routines.

- Read the words of Jesus and the proverb, sharing how each of those verses helped you think about rhythms.

- Ask each other about the lists, activities, and intentional times of rest you identified in the *On Your Own* section on the previous pages. Pay attention to your wife's natural rhythms and those that she desires.

- Complete the *Our Rhythms* section below, identifying ways that you can be intentional with your time as individuals, as a couple, and as a family. (You may want to do this now while it's fresh, or after the video when you have some more input from your video mentors.)

- Go to *Love That Lasts* in your library at *bethkeworkshops.com* and watch this week's video: Rhythms with John Mark and Tammy Comer. Then, ask each other what was most interesting, most challenging, and a big takeaway from the video. Use the video sidebar to take notes and to help your conversation.

- Finish your time together by identifying a favorite or most helpful takeaway from each of the past 12 sessions. As you do, consider how what you've experienced can become a natural part of your rhythm in love and marriage.

- If you're not yet in community with other Christians, don't rob yourself of this incredible joy. Your church community truly is the next most important relationship in your life next to your marriage. Remember, God created us for relationships. You need people around you to share the joys and the struggles of faith—people who will encourage you in your rhythms as the days, weeks, months, and years roll along. God's people are His masterpiece. His church is His bride. He made you for love. Everybody wants a love that lasts.

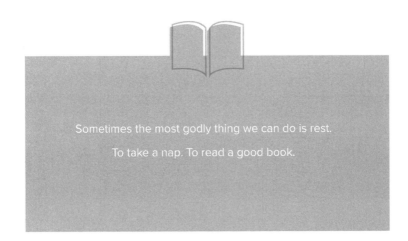

Sometimes the most godly thing we can do is rest.
To take a nap. To read a good book.

Rhythms with

John Mark & Tammy Comer

This section is a place to take notes if you also purchased the 12 corresponding video sessions from our 12 mentors. What did they say that resonated with you? What was your favorite part? What was most challenging?

_____

_____

_____

_____

_____

_____

_____

_____

_____

_____

_____

_____

_____

_____

_____

If you don't have this video
you can purchase it at

lovethatlasts.co/videoseries

OUR RHYTHMS

Write down things that are needed for a healthy rhythm as individuals, a couple, and as a family. Then, identify times within your daily or weekly schedule that you can intentionally prioritize the things that everyone needs in their healthy rhythms. (For example, if you need to spend 20 minutes reading your Bible and praying by yourself, and the best time to be alone is at 6am, then mark those down.) Identify as many or as few as you need to right now. This is just another tool to help you start thinking intentionally about establishing healthy rhythms in your life!

	NEEDS	TIME
HUSBAND		
WIFE		
COUPLE		
FAMILY		

1. Theology of Marriage: _____

2. Trust: _____

3. Communication: _____

4. Conflict: _____

5. Faith: _____

6. Purpose: _____

7. Sex: _____

8. Parenting: _____

9. Finances: _____

10. Boundaries: _____

11. Addiction: _____

12. Rhythms: _____

Let us know what you think! We'd love to hear from you!

#LoveThatLasts

A Final Word to Our Friends

You made it! Congrats! We know it wasn't easy. First, we wanted to extend a genuine and heartfelt thank you for taking this journey with us.

Second, we'd love to hear your feedback. You can say hi at our social links below, or if you use the hashtag #LoveThatLasts, we tend to click on that every so often and hop in the conversation with you.

We pray that you were encouraged as you went through them. I know they were deeply encouraging for us to write and work through. There's nothing like the power of grace and the love of Jesus to revitalize or strengthen any relationship out there. And don't forget that the secret of a healthy marriage, grace, is less like a flu shot and more like oxygen. It's something we need every second of every day to succeed, not just something we find once and then never come back for.

So rest in God's grace and love for you and your spouse (or significant other). He sees you. He knows you. He is with you.

Jeff & Alyssa

JEFF

@jeffersonbethke
@jeffersonbethke
fb.com/jeffersonbethkepage

ALYSSA

@alyssajoybethke
@alyssajoybethke
fb.com/alyssajoybethke

#LoveThatLasts

One of the secrets to a healthy relationship is it needs to be fed for it to grow. No relationship becomes healthy, vibrant, or joyful from complacency. In fact, the minute proactivity leaves the relationship is the minute it can begin to breakdown. In *31 Creative Ways to Love* and *Encourage Him and Her*, Jefferson and Alyssa Bethke lay out simple ways to bring the beauty, joy, and vibrancy back to a relationship. Each day brings a new adventure that can range from being serious to whimsical to humerous. Take this one month journey with your significant other and come out the other side with a stronger and more healthy relationship than before.

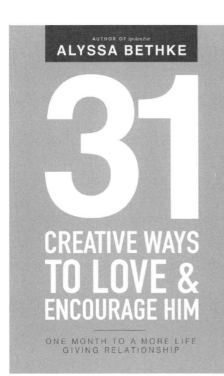

GET $10 OFF

(normally $32.99 for the bundle)

at shop.jeffandalyssa.com

by using code

"LOVETHATLASTS"

at checkout.

START A MARRIAGE SMALL GROUP

You can do the *Love That Lasts*

journey in a group setting.

Average is $60 per couple.

(Normal price is $144.)

Start your group at

shop.jeffandalyssa.com.